Elizabeth Barrett Browning

# The Poetical Works Of Ellizabeth Barrrett Browning - Vol-Iv

Elizabeth Barrett Browning

**The Poetical Works Of Ellizabeth Barrrett Browning - Vol-Iv**

ISBN/EAN: 9783742842701

Manufactured in Europe, USA, Canada, Australia, Japa

Cover: Foto ©ninafisch / pixelio.de

Manufactured and distributed by brebook publishing software (www.brebook.com)

Elizabeth Barrett Browning

The Poetical Works Of Ellizabeth Barrrett Browning - Vol-Iv

# CONTENTS.

POEMS:—

|  | PAGE |
|---|---|
| A Child's Grave at Florence | 3 |
| Catarina to Camoens | 12 |
| Life and Love | 20 |
| A Denial | 22 |
| Proof and Disproof | 25 |
| Question and Answer | 29 |
| Inclusions | 30 |
| Insufficiency | 32 |

SONNETS FROM THE PORTUGUESE . . . . 33

CASA GUIDI WINDOWS:—

| First Part | 83 |
|---|---|
| Second Part | 134 |

POEMS BEFORE CONGRESS:—

| Napoleon III. in Italy | 171 |
|---|---|
| The Dance | 190 |
| A Tale of Villafranca | 195 |
| A Court Lady | 200 |

POEMS BEFORE CONGRESS—*continued*

| | PAGE |
|---|---|
| AN AUGUST VOICE | 207 |
| CHRISTMAS GIFTS | 213 |
| ITALY AND THE WORLD | 217 |
| A CURSE FOR A NATION | 227 |

LAST POEMS:—

| | |
|---|---|
| LITTLE MATTIE | 241 |
| A FALSE STEP | 246 |
| VOID IN LAW | 248 |
| LORD WALTER'S WIFE | 252 |
| BIANCA AMONG THE NIGHTINGALES | 259 |
| MY KATE | 267 |
| A SONG FOR THE RAGGED SCHOOLS OF LONDON | 270 |
| MAY'S LOVE | 279 |
| AMY'S CRUELTY | 280 |
| MY HEART AND I | 284 |
| THE BEST THING IN THE WORLD | 287 |
| WHERE'S AGNES? | 288 |

# POEMS

IV.

# A CHILD'S GRAVE AT FLORENCE.

### A.A.E.C.

### BORN, JULY 1848.   DIED, NOVEMBER 1849.

### I.

OF English blood, of Tuscan birth,
 What country should we give her?
Instead of any on the earth,
 The civic Heavens receive her.

### II.

And here among the English tombs
 In Tuscan ground we lay her,
While the blue Tuscan sky endomes
 Our English words of prayer.

III.

A little child!—how long she lived,
　By months, not years, is reckoned:
Born in one July, she survived
　Alone to see a second.

IV.

Bright-featured, as the July sun
　Her little face still played in,
And splendours, with her birth begun,
　Had had no time for fading.

V.

So, LILY, from those July hours,
　No wonder we should call her;
She looked such kinship to the flowers,—
　Was but a little taller.

VI.

A Tuscan Lily,—only white,
　As Dante, in abhorrence
Of red corruption, wished aright
　The lilies of his Florence.

### VII.

We could not wish her whiter,—her
    Who perfumed with pure blossom
The house—a lovely thing to wear
    Upon a mother's bosom!

### VIII.

This July creature thought perhaps
    Our speech not worth assuming;
She sat upon her parents' laps
    And mimicked the gnat's humming;

### IX.

Said "father," "mother"—then left off,
    For tongues celestial, fitter:
Her hair had grown just long enough
    To catch heaven's jasper-glitter.

### X.

Babes! Love could always hear and see
    Behind the cloud that hid them.
"Let little children come to Me,
    And do not thou forbid them."

### XI.

So, unforbidding, have we met,
   And gently here have laid her,
Though winter is no time to get
   The flowers that should o'erspread her:

### XII.

We should bring pansies quick with spring,
   Rose, violet, daffodilly,
And also, above everything,
   White lilies for our Lily.

### XIII.

Nay, more than flowers, this grave exacts,—
   Glad, grateful attestations
Of her sweet eyes and pretty acts,
   With calm renunciations.

### XIV.

Her very mother with light feet
   Should leave the place too earthy,
Saying "The angels have thee, Sweet,
   Because we are not worthy.'

XV.

But winter kills the orange-buds,
    The gardens in the frost are,
And all the heart dissolves in floods,
    Remembering we have lost her.

XVI.

Poor earth, poor heart,—too weak, too weak
    To miss the July shining!
Poor heart!—what bitter words we speak
    When God speaks of resigning!

XVII.

Sustain this heart in us that faints,
    Thou God, the self-existent!
We catch up wild at parting saints
    And feel Thy heaven too distant.

XVIII.

The wind that swept them out of sin
    Has ruffled all our vesture:
On the shut door that let them in
    We beat with frantic gesture,—

### XIX.

To us, us also, open straight!
    The outer life is chilly;
Are *we* too, like the earth, to wait
    Till next year for our Lily?

### XX.

—Oh, my own baby on my knees,
    My leaping, dimpled treasure,
At every word I write like these,
    Clasped close with stronger pressure!

### XXI.

Too well my own heart understands,—
    At every word beats fuller—
My little feet, my little hands,
    And hair of Lily's colour!

### XXII.

But God gives patience, Love learns strength,
    And Faith remembers promise,
And Hope itself can smile at length
    On other hopes gone from us.

### XXIII.

Love, strong as Death, shall conquer Death,
    Through struggle made more glorious:
This mother stills her sobbing breath,
    Renouncing yet victorious.

### XXIV.

Arms, empty of her child, she lifts
    With spirit unbereaven,—
"God will not all take back His gifts;
    My Lily's mine in heaven.

### XXV.

"Still mine! maternal rights serene
    Not given to another!
The crystal bars shine faint between
    The souls of child and mother.

### XXVI.

"Meanwhile," the mother cries, "content!
    Our love was well divided:
Its sweetness following where she went,
    Its anguish stayed where I did.

XXVII.

"Well done of God, to halve the lot,
    And give her all the sweetness;
To us, the empty room and cot,—
    To her, the Heaven's completeness.


XXVIII.

"To us, this grave,—to her, the rows
    The mystic palm-trees spring in;
To us, the silence in the house,—
    To her, the choral singing.


XXIX.

"For her, to gladden in God's view,—
    For us, to hope and bear on.
Grow, Lily, in thy garden new,
    Beside the Rose of Sharon!


XXX.

"Grow fast in heaven, sweet Lily clipped,
    In love more calm than this is,
And may the angels dewy-lipped
    Remind thee of our kisses!

### XXXI.

"While none shall tell thee of our tears,
　These human tears now falling,
Till, after a few patient years,
　One home shall take us all in.

### XXXII.

"Child, father, mother—who, left out?
　Not mother, and not father!
And when, our dying couch about,
　The natural mists shall gather,

### XXXIII.

"Some smiling angel close shall stand
　In old Correggio's fashion,
And bear a LILY in his hand,
　For death's ANNUNCIATION."

## CATARINA TO CAMOENS

(DYING IN HIS ABSENCE ABROAD, AND REFERRING TO THE POEM IN WHICH HE RECORDED THE SWEETNESS OF HER EYES).

### I.

On the door you will not enter,
   I have gazed too long: adieu!
Hope withdraws her peradventure;
   Death is near me,—and not *you*.
      Come, O lover,
      Close and cover
These poor eyes, you called, I ween,
"Sweetest eyes were ever seen!"

### II.

When I heard you sing that burden
   In my vernal days and bowers,
Other praises disregarding,
   I but hearkened that of yours—

Only saying
In heart-playing,
"Blessed eyes mine eyes have been,
If the sweetest HIS have seen!"

### III.

But all changes. At this vesper,
  Cold the sun shines down the door.
If you stood there, would you whisper
  "Love, I love you," as before,—
    Death pervading
    Now, and shading
Eyes you sang of, that yestreen,
As the sweetest ever seen?

### IV.

Yes. I think, were you beside them,
  Near the bed I die upon,
Though their beauty you denied them,
  As you stood there, looking down,
    You would truly
    Call them duly,
For the love's sake found therein,
"Sweetest eyes were ever seen."

V.

And if *you* looked down upon them,
 And if *they* looked up to *you*,
All the light which has foregone them
 Would be gathered back anew:
  They would truly
  Be as duly
Love-transformed to beauty's sheen,
"Sweetest eyes were ever seen."

VI.

But, ah me! you only see me,
 In your thoughts of loving man,
Smiling soft perhaps and dreamy
 Through the wavings of my fan;
  And unweeting
  Go repeating,
In your reverie serene,
"Sweetest eyes were ever seen——"

VII.

While my spirit leans and reaches
 From my body still and pale,
Fain to hear what tender speech is
 In your love to help my bale.

O my poet,
  Come and show it!
Come, of latest love, to glean
"Sweetest eyes were ever seen."

### VIII.

O my poet, O my prophet,
  When you praised their sweetness so,
Did you think, in singing of it,
  That it might be near to go?
    Had you fancies
    From their glances,
That the grave would quickly screen
"Sweetest eyes were ever seen"?

### IX.

No reply. The fountain's warble
  In the courtyard sounds alone.
As the water to the marble
  So my heart falls with a moan
    From love-sighing
    To this dying.
Death forerunneth Love to win
"Sweetest eyes were ever seen."

### X.

*Will* you come? When I'm departed
   Where all sweetnesses are hid,
Where thy voice, my tender-hearted,
   Will not lift up either lid.
      Cry, O lover,
      Love is over!
Cry, beneath the cypress green,
"Sweetest eyes were ever seen!"

### XI.

When the angelus is ringing,
   Near the convent will you walk,
And recall the choral singing
   Which brought angels down our talk?
      Spirit-shriven
      I viewed Heaven,
Till you smiled—"Is earth unclean,
Sweetest eyes were ever seen?"

### XII.

When beneath the palace-lattice
   You ride slow as you have done,
And you see a face there that is
   Not the old familiar one,—

Will you oftly
Murmur softly,
"Here ye watched me morn and e'en,
Sweetest eyes were ever seen!"

### XIII.

When the palace-ladies, sitting
  Round your gittern, shall have said,
"Poet, sing those verses written
  For the lady who is dead,"
    Will you tremble
    Yet dissemble,—
Or sing hoarse, with tears between,
"Sweetest eyes were ever seen"?

### XIV.

"Sweetest eyes!" how sweet in flowings
  The repeated cadence is!
Though you sang a hundred poems,
  Still the best one would be this.
    I can hear it
    'Twixt my spirit
And the earth-noise intervene—
"Sweetest eyes were ever seen!"

XV.

But the priest waits for the praying,
    And the choir are on their knees,
And the soul must pass away in
    Strains more solemn-high than these.
    *Miserere*
    For the weary!
Oh, no longer for Catrine
"Sweetest eyes were ever seen!"


XVI.

Keep my riband, take and keep it,
    (I have loosed it from my hair)*
Feeling, while you overweep it,
    Not alone in your despair,
        Since with saintly
        Watch unfaintly
Out of heaven shall o'er you lean
"Sweetest eyes were ever seen."


XVII.

But—but *now*—yet unremovèd
    Up to heaven, they glisten fast;

---

\* She left him the riband from her hair

You may cast away, Belovèd,
  In your future all my past:
    Such old phrases
    May be praises
For some fairer bosom-queen—
"Sweetest eyes were ever seen!"

### XVIII.

Eyes of mine, what are ye doing?
  Faithless, faithless,—praised amiss
If a tear be of your showing,
  Dropt for any hope of HIS!
    Death has boldness
    Besides coldness,
If unworthy tears demean
"Sweetest eyes were ever seen."

### XIX.

I will look out to his future;
  I will bless it till it shine.
Should he ever be a suitor
  Unto sweeter eyes than mine,
    Sunshine gild them,
    Angels shield them,
Whatsoever eyes terrene
*Be* the sweetest HIS have seen!

## *LIFE AND LOVE.*

### I.

FAST this Life of mine was dying,
   Blind already and calm as death,
Snowflakes on her bosom lying
   Scarcely heaving with her breath.

### II.

Love came by, and having known her
   In a dream of fabled lands,
Gently stooped, and laid upon her
   Mystic chrism of holy hands;

### III.

Drew his smile across her folded
   Eyelids, as the swallow dips;
Breathed as finely as the cold did
   Through the locking of her lips.

IV.

So, when Life looked upward, being
    Warmed and breathed on from above,
What sight could she have for seeing,
    Evermore . . . but only LOVE?

## A DENIAL.

### I.

WE have met late—it is too late to meet,
    O friend, not more than friend!
Death's forecome shroud is tangled round my feet,
And if I step or stir, I touch the end.
    In this last jeopardy
Can I approach thee, I, who cannot move?
How shall I answer thy request for love?
    Look in my face and see.

### II.

I love thee not, I dare not love thee! go
    In silence; drop my hand.
If thou seek roses, seek them where they blow
In garden-alleys, not in desert-sand.
    Can life and death agree,
That thou shouldst stoop thy song to my complaint?
I cannot love thee. If the word is faint,
    Look in my face and see.

### III.

I might have loved thee in some former days.
    Oh, then, my spirits had leapt
As now they sink, at hearing thy love-praise!
Before these faded cheeks were overwept,
    Had this been asked of me,
To love thee with my whole strong heart and head,—
I should have said still . . . yes, but *smiled* and said,
    "Look in my face and see!"

### IV.

But now . . God sees me, God, who took my heart
    And drowned it in life's surge.
In all your wide warm earth I have no part—
A light song overcomes me like a dirge.
    Could Love's great harmony
The saints keep step to when their bonds are loose,
Not weigh me down? am *I* a wife to choose?
    Look in my face and see—

### V.

While I behold, as plain as one who dreams,
    Some woman of full worth,
Whose voice, as cadenced as a silver stream's,
Shall prove the fountain-soul which sends it forth;

One younger, more thought-free
And fair and gay, than I, thou must forget,
With brighter eyes than these . . which are not wet . .
    Look in my face and see!


### VI.

So farewell thou, whom I have known too late
    To let thee come so near.
Be counted happy while men call thee great,
And one belovèd woman feels thee dear!—
    Not I!—that cannot be.
I am lost, I am changed,—I must go farther, where
The change shall take me worse, and no one dare
    Look in my face and see.


### VII.

Meantime I bless thee. By these thoughts of mine
    I bless thee from all such!
I bless thy lamp to oil, thy cup to wine,
Thy hearth to joy, thy hand to an equal touch
    Of loyal troth. For me,
I love thee not, I love thee not!—away!
Here's no more courage in my soul to say
    "Look in my face and see."

## PROOF AND DISPROOF.

### I.

Dost thou love me, my Belovèd?
   Who shall answer yes or no?
What is provèd or disprovèd
   When my soul inquireth so,
Dost thou love me, my Belovèd?

### II.

I have seen thy heart to-day,
   Never open to the crowd,
While to love me aye and aye
   Was the vow as it was vowed
By thine eyes of steadfast grey.

### III.

Now I sit alone, alone—
   And the hot tears break and burn,
Now, Belovèd, thou art gone,
   Doubt and terror have their turn.
*Is* it love that I have known?

### IV.

I have known some bitter things,—
   Anguish, anger, solitude.
Year by year an evil brings,
   Year by year denies a good;
March winds violate my springs.

### V.

I have known how sickness bends,
   I have known how sorrow breaks,—
How quick hopes have sudden ends,
   How the heart thinks till it aches
Of the smile of buried friends.

### VI.

Last, I have known *thee*, my brave
   Noble thinker, lover, doer!
The best knowledge last I have.
   But thou comest as the thrower
Of fresh flowers upon a grave.

### VII.

Count what feelings used to move me!
   Can this love assort with those?
Thou, who art so far above me,
   Wilt thou stoop so, for repose?
Is it true that thou canst love me?

### VIII.

Do not blame me if I doubt thee.
   I can call love by its name
When thine arm is wrapt about me;
   But even love seems not the same,
When I sit alone, without thee.

## IX.

In thy clear eyes I descried
    Many a proof of love, to-day;
But to-night, those unbelied
    Speechful eyes being gone away,
There's the proof to seek, beside.

## X.

Dost thou love me, my Belovèd?
    Only *thou* canst answer yes!
And, thou gone, the proof's disprovèd,
    And the cry rings answerless—
Dost thou love me, my Belovèd?

## QUESTION AND ANSWER.

### I.

LOVE you seek for, presupposes
   Summer heat and sunny glow.
Tell me, do you find moss-roses
   Budding, blooming in the snow?
Snow might kill the rose-tree's root—
Shake it quickly from your foot,
   Lest it harm you as you go.

### II.

From the ivy where it dapples
   A grey ruin, stone by stone,
Do you look for grapes or apples,
   Or for sad green leaves alone?
Pluck the leaves off, two or three—
Keep them for morality
   When you shall be safe and gone.

## INCLUSIONS.

### I.

Oh, wilt thou have my hand, Dear, to lie along in thine?
As a little stone in a running stream, it seems to lie and
    pine.
Now drop the poor pale hand, Dear, unfit to plight with
    thine.

### II.

Oh, wilt thou have my cheek, Dear, drawn closer to
    thine own?
My cheek is white, my cheek is worn, by many a tear
    run down.
Now leave a little space, Dear, lest it should wet thine
    own.

III.

Oh, must thou have my soul, Dear, commingled with
 thy soul?—
Red grows the cheek, and warm the hand; the part is
 in the whole:
Nor hands nor cheeks keep separate, when soul is joined
 to soul.

## INSUFFICIENCY.

### I.

THERE is no one beside thee and no one above thee,
    Thou standest alone as the nightingale sings !
    And my words that would praise thee are impotent things,
For none can express thee though all should approve thee.
    I love thee so, Dear, that I only can love thee.

### II.

Say, what can I do for thee? weary thee, grieve thee?
    Lean on thy shoulder, new burdens to add?
    Weep my tears over thee, making thee sad?
Oh, hold me not—love me not ! let me retrieve thee.
    I love thee so, Dear, that I only can leave thee.

# SONNETS

# FROM THE PORTUGUESE

## I.

I THOUGHT once how Theocritus had sung
Of the sweet years, the dear and wished-for years,
Who each one in a gracious hand appears
To bear a gift for mortals, old or young:
And, as I mused it in his antique tongue,
I saw, in gradual vision through my tears,
The sweet, sad years, the melancholy years,
Those of my own life, who by turns had flung
A shadow across me. Straightway I was 'ware,
So weeping, how a mystic Shape did move
Behind me, and drew me backward by the hair;
And a voice said in mastery, while I strove,—
"Guess now who holds thee?"—"Death," I said.
    But, there,
The silver answer rang,—"Not Death, but Love."

II.

But only three in all God's universe
Have heard this word thou hast said,—Himself, beside
Thee speaking, and me listening! and replied
One of us . . . *that* was God, . . . and laid the curse
So darkly on my eyelids, as to amerce
My sight from seeing thee,—that if I had died,
The deathweights, placed there, would have signified
Less absolute exclusion. "Nay" is worse
From God than from all others, O my friend!
Men could not part us with their worldly jars,
Nor the seas change us, nor the tempests bend;
Our hands would touch for all the mountain-bars:
And, heaven being rolled between us at the end,
We should but vow the faster for the stars.

### III.

UNLIKE are we, unlike, O princely Heart!
Unlike our uses and our destinies.
Our ministering two angels look surprise
On one another, as they strike athwart
Their wings in passing.  Thou, bethink thee, art
A guest for queens to social pageantries,
With gages from a hundred brighter eyes
Than tears even can make mine, to play thy part
Of chief musician.  What hast *thou* to do
With looking from the lattice-lights at me,
A poor, tired, wandering singer, singing through
The dark, and leaning up a cypress tree?
The chrism is on thine head,—on mine, the dew,—
And Death must dig the level where these agree.

IV.

Thou hast thy calling to some palace-floor,
Most gracious singer of high poems! where
The dancers will break footing, from the care
Of watching up thy pregnant lips for more.
And dost thou lift this house's latch too poor
For hand of thine? and canst thou think and bear
To let thy music drop here unaware
In folds of golden fulness at my door?
Look up and see the casement broken in,
The bats and owlets builders in the roof!
My cricket chirps against thy mandolin.
Hush, call no echo up in further proof
Of desolation! there's a voice within
That weeps . . as thou must sing . . alone, aloof.

## V.

I LIFT my heavy heart up solemnly,
As once Electra her sepulchral urn,
And, looking in thine eyes, I overturn
The ashes at thy feet.  Behold and see
What a great heap of grief lay hid in me,
And how the red wild sparkles dimly burn
Through the ashen greyness.  If thy foot in scorn
Could tread them out to darkness utterly,
It might be well perhaps.  But if instead
Thou wait beside me for the wind to blow
The grey dust up, . . . those laurels on thine head,
O my Belovèd, will not shield thee so,
That none of all the fires shall scorch and shred
The hair beneath.  Stand further off then! go.

### VI.

Go from me. Yet I feel that I shall stand
Henceforward in thy shadow. Nevermore
Alone upon the threshold of my door
Of individual life, I shall command
The uses of my soul, nor lift my hand
Serenely in the sunshine as before,
Without the sense of that which I forbore—
Thy touch upon the palm. The widest land
Doom takes to part us, leaves thy heart in mine
With pulses that beat double. What I do
And what I dream include thee, as the wine
Must taste of its own grapes. And when I sue
God for myself, He hears that name of thine,
And sees within my eyes the tears of two.

## VII.

THE face of all the world is changed, I think,
Since first I heard the footsteps of thy soul
Move still, oh, still, beside me, as they stole
Betwixt me and the dreadful outer brink
Of obvious death, where I, who thought to sink,
Was caught up into love, and taught the whole
Of life in a new rhythm. The cup of dole
God gave for baptism, I am fain to drink,
And praise its sweetness, Sweet, with thee anear.
The names of country, heaven, are changed away
For where thou art or shalt be, there or here;
And this . . this lute and song . . loved yesterday,
(The singing angels know) are only dear
Because thy name moves right in what they say.

VIII.

What can I give thee back, O liberal
And princely giver, who hast brought the gold
And purple of thine heart, unstained, untold
And laid them on the outside of the wall
For such as I to take or leave withal,
In unexpected largesse? am I cold,
Ungrateful, that for these most manifold
High gifts, I render nothing back at all?
Not so; not cold,—but very poor instead.
Ask God who knows. For frequent tears have run
The colours from my life, and left so dead
And pale a stuff, it were not fitly done
To give the same as pillow to thy head.
Go farther! let it serve to trample on.

## IX.

CAN it be right to give what I can give?
To let thee sit beneath the fall of tears
As salt as mine, and hear the sighing years
Re-sighing on my lips renunciative
Through those infrequent smiles which fail to live
For all thy adjurations? O my fears,
That this can scarce be right! We are not peers,
So to be lovers; and I own, and grieve,
That givers of such gifts as mine are, must
Be counted with the ungenerous. Out, alas!
I will not soil thy purple with my dust,
Nor breathe my poison on thy Venice-glass,
Nor give thee any love—which were unjust.
Beloved, I only love thee! let it pass.

## X.

YET, love, mere love, is beautiful indeed
And worthy of acceptation. Fire is bright,
Let temple burn, or flax; an equal light
Leaps in the flame from cedar-plank or weed:
And love is fire. And when I say at need
*I love thee* . . mark! . . *I love thee*—in thy sight
I stand transfigured, glorified aright,
With conscience of the new rays that proceed
Out of my face toward thine. There's nothing low
In love, when love the lowest: meanest creatures
Who love God, God accepts while loving so.
And what I *feel*, across the inferior features
Of what I *am*, doth flash itself, and show
How that great work of Love enhances Nature's.

## XI.

And therefore if to love can be desert,
I am not all unworthy. Cheeks as pale
As these you see, and trembling knees that fail
To bear the burden of a heavy heart,—
This weary minstrel-life that once was girt
To climb Aornus, and can scarce avail
To pipe now 'gainst the valley nightingale
A melancholy music,—why advert
To these things? O Belovèd, it is plain
I am not of thy worth nor for thy place!
And yet, because I love thee, I obtain
From that same love this vindicating grace,
To live on still in love, and yet in vain,—
To bless thee, yet renounce thee to thy face.

### XII.

INDEED this very love which is my boast,
And which, when rising up from breast to brow,
Doth crown me with a ruby large enow
To draw men's eyes and prove the inner cost,—
This love even, all my worth, to the uttermost,
I should not love withal, unless that thou
Hadst set me an example, shown me how,
When first thine earnest eyes with mine were crossed,
And love called love. And thus, I cannot speak
Of love even, as a good thing of my own:
Thy soul hath snatched up mine all faint and weak,
And placed it by thee on a golden throne,—
And that I love (O soul, we must be meek!)
Is by thee only, whom I love alone.

### XIII.

AND wilt thou have me fashion into speech
The love I bear thee, finding words enough,
And hold the torch out, while the winds are rough,
Between our faces, to cast light on each?—
I drop it at thy feet. I cannot teach
My hand to hold my spirit so far off
From myself—me—that I should bring thee proof
In words, of love hid in me out of reach.
Nay, let the silence of my womanhood
Commend my woman-love to thy belief,—
Seeing that I stand unwon, however wooed,
And rend the garment of my life, in brief,
By a most dauntless, voiceless fortitude,
Lest one touch of this heart convey its grief.

## XIV.

If thou must love me, let it be for nought
Except for love's sake only. Do not say
" I love her for her smile—her look—her way
Of speaking gently,—for a trick of thought
That falls in well with mine, and certes brought
A sense of pleasant ease on such a day "—
For these things in themselves, Belovèd, may
Be changed, or change for thee,—and love, so wrought,
May be unwrought so. Neither love me for
Thine own dear pity's wiping my cheeks dry,—
A creature might forget to weep, who bore
Thy comfort long, and lose thy love thereby!
But love me for love's sake, that evermore
Thou mayst love on, through love's eternity.

## XV.

Accuse me not, beseech thee, that I wear
Too calm and sad a face in front of thine;
For we two look two ways, and cannot shine
With the same sunlight on our brow and hair.
On me thou lookest with no doubting care,
As on a bee shut in a crystalline;
Since sorrow hath shut me safe in love's divine,
And to spread wing and fly in the outer air
Were most impossible failure, if I strove
To fail so. But I look on thee—on thee—
Beholding, besides love, the end of love,
Hearing oblivion beyond memory;
As one who sits and gazes from above,
Over the rivers to the bitter sea.

### XVI.

AND yet, because thou overcomest so,
Because thou art more noble and like a king,
Thou canst prevail against my fears and fling
Thy purple round me, till my heart shall grow
Too close against thine heart henceforth to know
How it shook when alone. Why, conquering
May prove as lordly and complete a thing
In lifting upward, as in crushing low!
And as a vanquished soldier yields his sword
To one who lifts him from the bloody earth,
Even so, Belovèd, I at last record,
Here ends my strife. If *thou* invite me forth,
I rise above abasement at the word.
Make thy love larger to enlarge my worth.

## XVII.

My poet, thou canst touch on all the notes
God set between His After and Before,
And strike up and strike off the general roar
Of the rushing worlds a melody that floats
In a serene air purely. Antidotes
Of medicated music, answering for
Mankind's forlornest uses, thou canst pour
From thence into their ears. |God's will devotes
Thine to such ends, and mine to wait on thine.
How, Dearest, wilt thou have me for most use?
A hope, to sing by gladly? or a fine
Sad memory, with thy songs to interfuse?
A shade, in which to sing—of palm or pine?
A grave, on which to rest from singing? Choose.

## XVIII.

I NEVER gave a lock of hair away
To a man, Dearest, except this to thee,
Which now upon my fingers thoughtfully,
I ring out to the full brown length and say
"Take it." My day of youth went yesterday;
My hair no longer bounds to my foot's glee,
Nor plant I it from rose or myrtle-tree,
As girls do, any more: it only may
Now shade on two pale cheeks the mark of tears,
Taught drooping from the head that hangs aside
Through sorrow's trick. I thought the funeral-shears
Would take this first, but Love is justified,—
Take it thou,—finding pure, from all those years,
The kiss my mother left here when she died.

## XIX.

The soul's Rialto hath its merchandise;
I barter curl for curl upon that mart,
And from my poet's forehead to my heart
Receive this lock which outweighs argosies,—
As purply black, as erst to Pindar's eyes
The dim purpureal tresses gloomed athwart
The nine white Muse-brows.   For this counterpart, . .
The bay-crown's shade, Belovèd, I surmise,
Still lingers on thy curl, it is so black!
Thus, with a fillet of smooth-kissing breath,
I tie the shadows safe from gliding back,
And lay the gift where nothing hindereth;
Here on my heart, as on thy brow, to lack
No natural heat till mine grows cold in death.

### XX.

BELOVED, my Belovèd, when I think
That thou wast in the world a year ago,
What time I sat alone here in the snow
And saw no footprint, heard the silence sink
No moment at thy voice, but, link by link,
Went counting all my chains as if that so
They never could fall off at any blow
Struck by thy possible hand,—why, thus I drink
Of life's great cup of wonder! Wonderful,
Never to feel thee thrill the day or night
With personal act or speech,—nor ever cull
Some prescience of thee with the blossoms white
Thou sawest growing! Atheists are as dull,
Who cannot guess God's presence out of sight.

### XXI.

Say over again, and yet once over again,
That thou dost love me. Though the word repeated
Should seem "a cuckoo-song," as thou dost treat it.
Remember, never to the hill or plain,
Valley and wood, without her cuckoo-strain
Comes the fresh Spring in all her green completed.
Belovèd, I, amid the darkness greeted
By a doubtful spirit-voice, in that doubt's pain
Cry, "Speak once more—thou lovest!" Who can fear
Too many stars, though each in heaven shall roll,
Too many flowers, though each shall crown the year?
Say thou dost love me, love me, love me—toll
The silver iterance!—only minding, Dear,
To love me also in silence with thy soul.

## XXII.

When our two souls stand up erect and strong,
Face to face, silent, drawing nigh and nigher,
Until the lengthening wings break into fire
At either curvèd point,—what bitter wrong
Can the earth do to us, that we should not long
Be here contented? Think. In mounting higher,
The angels would press on us and aspire
To drop some golden orb of perfect song
Into our deep, dear silence. Let us stay
Rather on earth, Belovèd,—where the unfit
Contrarious moods of men recoil away
And isolate pure spirits, and permit
A place to stand and love in for a day,
With darkness and the death-hour rounding it.

### XXIII.

Is it indeed so? If I lay here dead,
Wouldst thou miss any life in losing mine?
And would the sun for thee more coldly shine
Because of grave-damps falling round my head?
I marvelled, my Belovèd, when I read
Thy thought so in the letter. I am thine—
But . . . *so* much to thee? Can I pour thy wine
While my hands tremble? Then my soul, instead
Of dreams of death, resumes life's lower range.
Then, love me, Love! look on me—breathe on me!
As brighter ladies do not count it strange,
For love, to give up acres and degree,
I yield the grave for thy sake, and exchange
My near sweet view of Heaven, for earth with thee!

## XXIV.

LET the world's sharpness, like a clasping knife,
Shut in upon itself and do no harm
In this close hand of Love, now soft and warm,
And let us hear no sound of human strife
After the click of the shutting. Life to life—
I lean upon thee, Dear, without alarm,
And feel as safe as guarded by a charm
Against the stab of worldlings, who if rife
Are weak to injure. Very whitely still
The lilies of our lives may reassure
Their blossoms from their roots, accessible
Alone to heavenly dews that drop not fewer
Growing straight, out of man's reach, on the hill.
God only, who made us rich, can make us poor.

### XXV.

A HEAVY heart, Belovèd, have I borne
From year to year until I saw thy face,
And sorrow after sorrow took the place
Of all those natural joys as lightly worn
As the stringed pearls, each lifted in its turn
By a beating heart at dance-time.   Hopes apace
Were changed to long despairs, till God's own grace
Could scarcely lift above the world forlorn
My heavy heart.   Then *thou* didst bid me bring
And let it drop adown thy calmly great
Deep being!   Fast it sinketh, as a thing
Which its own nature doth precipitate,
While thine doth close above it, mediating
Betwixt the stars and the unaccomplished fate.

## XXVI.

I LIVED with visions for my company
Instead of men and women, years ago,
And found them gentle mates, nor thought to know
A sweeter music than they played to me.
But soon their trailing purple was not free
Of this world's dust, their lutes did silent grow,
And I myself grew faint and blind below
Their vanishing eyes. Then THOU didst come—to be,
Belovèd, what they seemed. Their shining fronts,
Their songs, their splendours (better, yet the same,
As river-water hallowed into fonts),
Met in thee, and from out thee overcame
My soul with satisfaction of all wants:
Because God's gifts put man's best dreams to shame.

## XXVII.

My own Belovèd, who hast lifted me
From this drear flat of earth where I was thrown,
And, in betwixt the languid ringlets, blown
A life-breath, till the forehead hopefully
Shines out again, as all the angels see,
Before thy saving kiss! My own, my own,
Who camest to me when the world was gone,
And I who looked for only God, found *thee!*
I find thee; I am safe, and strong, and glad.
As one who stands in dewless asphodel
Looks backward on the tedious time he had
In the upper life,—so I, with bosom-swell,
Make witness, here, between the good and bad,
That Love, as strong as Death, retrieves as well.

## XXVIII.

My letters! all dead paper, mute and white!
And yet they seem alive and quivering
Against my tremulous hands which loose the string
And let them drop down on my knee to-night.
This said,—he wished to have me in his sight
Once, as a friend: this fixed a day in spring
To come and touch my hand . . . a simple thing,
Yet I wept for it!—this, . . . the paper's light . . .
Said, *Dear, I love thee*; and I sank and quailed
As if God's future thundered on my past.
This said, *I am thine*—and so its ink has paled
With lying at my heart that beat too fast.
And this . . . O Love, thy words have ill availed
If, what this said, I dared repeat at last!

### XXIX.

I THINK of thee!—my thoughts do twine and bud
About thee, as wild vines, about a tree,
Put out broad leaves, and soon there 's nought to see
Except the straggling green which hides the wood.
Yet, O my palm-tree, be it understood
I will not have my thoughts instead of thee
Who art dearer, better!  Rather, instantly
Renew thy presence; as a strong tree should,
Rustle thy boughs and set thy trunk all bare,
And let these bands of greenery which insphere thee
Drop heavily down,—burst, shattered, everywhere!
Because, in this deep joy to see and hear thee
And breathe within thy shadow a new air,
I do not think of thee—I am too near thee.

### XXX.

I SEE thine image through my tears to-night,
And yet to-day I saw thee smiling. How
Refer the cause?—Belovèd, is it thou
Or I, who makes me sad? The acolyte
Amid the chanted joy and thankful rite
May so fall flat, with pale insensate brow,
On the altar-stair. I hear thy voice and vow,
Perplexed, uncertain, since thou art out of sight,
As he, in his swooning ears, the choir's Amen.
Belovèd, dost thou love? or did I see all
The glory as I dreamed, and fainted when
Too vehement light dilated my ideal,
For my soul's eyes? Will that light come again,
As now these tears come—falling hot and real?

## XXXI.

THOU comest! all is said without a word.
I sit beneath thy looks, as children do
In the noon-sun, with souls that tremble through
Their happy eyelids from an unaverred
Yet prodigal inward joy.  Behold, I erred
In that last doubt! and yet I cannot rue
The sin most, but the occasion—that we two
Should for a moment stand unministered
By a mutual presence.  Ah, keep near and close,
Thou dovelike help! and, when my fears would rise,
With thy broad heart serenely interpose:
Brood down with thy divine sufficiencies
These thoughts which tremble when bereft of those,
Like callow birds left desert to the skies.

## XXXII.

THE first time that the sun rose on thine oath
To love me, I looked forward to the moon
To slacken all those bonds which seemed too soon
And quickly tied to make a lasting troth.
Quick-loving hearts, I thought, may quickly loathe;
And, looking on myself, I seemed not one
For such man's love!—more like an out-of-tune
Worn viol, a good singer would be wroth
To spoil his song with, and which, snatched in haste,
Is laid down at the first ill-sounding note.
I did not wrong myself so, but I placed
A wrong on *thee*. For perfect strains may float
'Neath master-hands, from instruments defaced,—
And great souls, at one stroke, may do and doat.

### XXXIII.

Yes, call me by my pet-name! let me hear
The name I used to run at, when a child,
From innocent play, and leave the cowslips piled,
To glance up in some face that proved me dear
With the look of its eyes. I miss the clear
Fond voices which, being drawn and reconciled
Into the music of Heaven's undefiled,
Call me no longer. Silence on the bier,
While I call God—call God!—So let thy mouth
Be heir to those who are now exanimate.
Gather the north flowers to complete the south,
And catch the early love up in the late.
Yes, call me by that name,—and I, in truth,
With the same heart, will answer and not wait.

## XXXIV.

WITH the same heart, I said, I'll answer thee
As those, when thou shalt call me by my name—
Lo, the vain promise! is the same, the same,
Perplexed and ruffled by life's strategy?
When called before, I told how hastily
I dropped my flowers or brake off from a game,
To run and answer with the smile that came
At play last moment, and went on with me
Through my obedience.  When I answer now,
I drop a grave thought, break from solitude;
Yet still my heart goes to thee—ponder how—
Not as to a single good, but all my good!
Lay thy hand on it, best one, and allow
That no child's foot could run fast as this blood.

## XXXV.

IF I leave all for thee, wilt thou exchange
And be all to me?   Shall I never miss
Home-talk and blessing and the common kiss
That comes to each in turn, nor count it strange,
When I look up, to drop on a new range
Of walls and floors, another home than this?
Nay, wilt thou fill that place by me which is
Filled by dead eyes too tender to know change?
That's hardest.   If to conquer love, has tried,
To conquer grief, tries more, as all things prove;
For grief indeed is love and grief beside.
Alas, I have grieved so I am hard to love.
Yet love me—wilt thou?   Open thine heart wide,
And fold within the wet wings of thy dove.

## XXXVI.

When we met first and loved, I did not build
Upon the event with marble. Could it mean
To last, a love set pendulous between
Sorrow and sorrow? Nay, I rather thrilled,
Distrusting every light that seemed to gild
The onward path, and feared to overlean
A finger even. And, though I have grown serene
And strong since then, I think that God has willed
A still renewable fear . . . O love, O troth . . .
Lest these enclaspèd hands should never hold,
This mutual kiss drop down between us both
As an unowned thing, once the lips being cold.
And Love, be false! if *he*, to keep one oath,
Must lose one joy, by his life's star foretold.

### XXXVII.

PARDON, oh, pardon, that my soul should make,
Of all that strong divineness which I know
For thine and thee, an image only so
Formed of the sand, and fit to shift and break.
It is that distant years which did not take
Thy sovranty, recoiling with a blow,
Have forced my swimming brain to undergo
Their doubt and dread, and blindly to forsake
Thy purity of likeness and distort
Thy worthiest love to a worthless counterfeit:
As if a shipwrecked Pagan, safe in port,
His guardian sea-god to commemorate,
Should set a sculptured porpoise, gills a-snort
And vibrant tail, within the temple-gate.

## XXXVIII.

First time he kissed me, he but only kissed
The fingers of this hand wherewith I write;
And ever since, it grew more clean and white,
Slow to world-greetings, quick with its "Oh, list,"
When the angels speak. A ring of amethyst
I could not wear here, plainer to my sight,
Than that first kiss. The second passed in height
The first, and sought the forehead, and half missed,
Half falling on the hair. O beyond meed!
That was the chrism of love, which love's own crown,
With sanctifying sweetness, did precede.
The third upon my lips was folded down
In perfect, purple state; since when, indeed,
I have been proud and said, "My love, my own."

## XXXIX.

BECAUSE thou hast the power and own'st the grace
To look through and behind this mask of me
(Against which years have beat thus blanchingly
With their rains), and behold my soul's true face,
The dim and weary witness of life's race,—
Because thou hast the faith and love to see,
Through that same soul's distracting lethargy,
The patient angel waiting for a place
In the new Heavens,—because nor sin nor woe,
Nor God's infliction, nor death's neighbourhood,
Nor all which others viewing, turn to go,
Nor all which makes me tired of all, self-viewed,—
Nothing repels thee, . . . Dearest, teach me so
To pour out gratitude, as thou dost, good!

## XL.

Oh, yes! they love through all this world of ours!
I will not gainsay love, called love forsooth.
I have heard love talked in my early youth,
And since, not so long back but that the flowers
Then gathered, smell still. Mussulmans and Giaours
Throw kerchiefs at a smile, and have no ruth
For any weeping. Polypheme's white tooth
Slips on the nut if, after frequent showers,
The shell is over-smooth,—and not so much
Will turn the thing called love, aside to hate
Or else to oblivion. But thou art not such
A lover, my Belovèd! thou canst wait
Through sorrow and sickness, to bring souls to touch,
And think it soon when others cry "Too late."

### XLI.

I THANK all who have loved me in their hearts,
With thanks and love from mine. Deep thanks to all
Who paused a little near the prison-wall
To hear my music in its louder parts
Ere they went onward, each one to the mart's
Or temple's occupation, beyond call.
But thou, who, in my voice's sink and fall
When the sob took it, thy divinest Art's
Own instrument didst drop down at thy foot
To hearken what I said between my tears, . . .
Instruct me how to thank thee! Oh, to shoot
My soul's full meaning into future years,
That *they* should lend it utterance, and salute
Love that endures, from Life that disappears!

## XLII.

*" My future will not copy fair my past "* —
I wrote that once; and thinking at my side
My ministering life-angel justified
The word by his appealing look upcast
To the white throne of God, I turned at last,
And there, instead, saw thee, not unallied
To angels in thy soul! Then I, long tried
By natural ills, received the comfort fast,
While budding, at thy sight, my pilgrim's staff
Gave out green leaves with morning dews impearled.
I seek no copy now of life's first half:
Leave here the pages with long musing curled,
And write me new my future's epigraph,
New angel mine, unhoped for in the world!

### XLIII.

How do I love thee? Let me count the ways.
I love thee to the depth and breadth and height
My soul can reach, when feeling out of sight
For the ends of Being and ideal Grace.
I love thee to the level of everyday's
Most quiet need, by sun and candlelight.
I love thee freely, as men strive for Right;
I love thee purely, as they turn from Praise.
I love thee with the passion put to use
In my old griefs, and with my childhood's faith.
I love thee with a love I seemed to lose
With my lost saints,—I love thee with the breath,
Smiles, tears, of all my life!—and, if God choose,
I shall but love thee better after death.

### XLIV.

BELOVÈD, thou hast brought me many flowers
Plucked in the garden, all the summer through
And winter, and it seemed as if they grew
In this close room, nor missed the sun and showers.
So, in the like name of that love of ours,
Take back these thoughts which here unfolded too,
And which on warm and cold days I withdrew
From my heart's ground. Indeed, those beds and bowers
Be overgrown with bitter weeds and rue,
And wait thy weeding; yet here's eglantine,
Here's ivy!—take them, as I used to do
Thy flowers, and keep them where they shall not pine.
Instruct thine eyes to keep their colours true,
And tell thy soul their roots are left in mine.

# CASA GUIDI WINDOWS

A Poem,

IN TWO PARTS

# ADVERTISEMENT TO THE FIRST EDITION.

THIS poem contains the impressions of the writer upon events in Tuscany of which she was a witness. "From a window," the critic may demur. She bows to the objection in the very title of her work. No continuous narrative nor exposition of political philosophy is attempted by her. It is a simple story of personal impressions, whose only value is in the intensity with which they were received, as proving her warm affection for a beautiful and unfortunate country, and the sincerity with which they are related, as indicating her own good faith and freedom from partisanship.

Of the two parts of this poem, the first was written nearly three years ago, while the second resumes the actual situation of 1851. The discrepancy between the two parts is a sufficient guarantee to the public of the truthfulness of the writer, who, though she certainly escaped the epidemic "falling sickness" of enthusiasm for Pio Nono, takes shame upon herself that she believed, like a woman, some royal oaths, and lost sight of the probable consequences of some obvious popular defects. If the discrepancy should be painful to the reader, let him understand that to the writer it has been more so. But such discrepancies we are called upon to accept at every hour by the conditions of our nature, implying the interval between aspiration and performance, between faith and disillusion, between hope and fact.

> "O trusted broken prophecy,
> O richest fortune sourly crost,
> Born for the future, to the future lost!"

Nay, not lost to the future in this case. The future of Italy shall not be disinherited.

FLORENCE, 1851.

# CASA GUIDI WINDOWS.

## PART I.

I HEARD last night a little child go singing
  'Neath Casa Guidi windows, by the church,
*O bella libertà, O bella !*—stringing
  The same words still on notes he went in search
So high for, you concluded the upspringing
  Of such a nimble bird to sky from perch
Must leave the whole bush in a tremble green,
  And that the heart of Italy must beat,
While such a voice had leave to rise serene
  'Twixt church and palace of a Florence street:
A little child, too, who not long had been
  By mother's finger steadied on his feet,
And still *O bella libertà* he sang.

Then I thought, musing, of the innumerous
  Sweet songs which still for Italy outrang

From older singers' lips who sang not thus
    Exultingly and purely, yet, with pang
Fast sheathed in music, touched the heart of us
    So finely that the pity scarcely pained.
I thought how Filicaja led on others,
    Bewailers for their Italy enchained,
And how they called her childless among mothers,
    Widow of empires, ay, and scarce refrained
Cursing her beauty to her face, as brothers
    Might a shamed sister's,—"Had she been less fair
She were less wretched;"—how, evoking so
    From congregated wrong and heaped despair
Of men and women writhing under blow,
    Harrowed and hideous in a filthy lair,
Some personating Image wherein woe
    Was wrapt in beauty from offending much,
They called it Cybele, or Niobe,
    Or laid it corpse-like on a bier for such,
Where all the world might drop for Italy
    Those cadenced tears which burn not where they touch,—
" Juliet of nations, canst thou die as we?
    And was the violet crown that crowned thy head
So over-large, though new buds made it rough,
    It slipped down and across thine eyelids dead,
O sweet, fair Juliet?" Of such songs enough,

Too many of such complaints! behold, instead,
Void at Verona, Juliet's marble trough:*
  As void as that is, are all images
Men set between themselves and actual wrong,
  To catch the weight of pity, meet the stress
Of conscience,—since 't is easier to gaze long
  On mournful masks and sad effigies
Than on real, live, weak creatures crushed by strong.

For me who stand in Italy to-day
Where worthier poets stood and sang before,
  I kiss their footsteps yet their words gainsay.
I can but muse in hope upon this shore
  Of golden Arno as it shoots away
Through Florence' heart beneath her bridges four:
  Bent bridges, seeming to strain off like bows,
And tremble while the arrowy undertide
  Shoots on and cleaves the marble as it goes,
And strikes up palace-walls on either side,
  And froths the cornice out in glittering rows,
With doors and windows quaintly multiplied,
  And terrace-sweeps, and gazers upon all,
By whom if flower or kerchief were thrown out
  From any lattice there, the same would fall

---

* They show at Verona, as the tomb of Juliet, an empty trough of stone.

Into the river underneath, no doubt,
    It runs so close and fast 'twixt wall and wall.
How beautiful! the mountains from without
    In silence listen for the word said next.
What word will men say,—here where Giotto planted
    His campanile like an unperplexed
Fine question Heavenward, touching the things
        granted
    A noble people who, being greatly vexed
In act, in aspiration keep undaunted?
    What word will God say? Michel's Night and Day
And Dawn and Twilight wait in marble scorn *
    Like dogs upon a dunghill, couched on clay
From whence the Medicean stamp's outworn,
    The final putting off of all such sway
By all such hands, and freeing of the unborn
    In Florence and the great world outside Florence.
Three hundred years his patient statues wait
    In that small chapel of the dim Saint Lawrence:
Day's eyes are breaking bold and passionate
    Over his shoulder, and will flash abhorrence
On darkness and with level looks meet fate,

---

\* These famous statues recline in the Sagrestia Nuova, on the tombs of Giuliano de' Medici, third son of Lorenzo the Magnificent, and Lorenzo of Urbino, his grandson. Strozzi's epigram on the Night, with Michel Angelo's rejoinder, is well known.

When once loose from that marble film of theirs :
The Night has wild dreams in her sleep, the Dawn
  Is haggard as the sleepless, Twilight wears
A sort of horror ; as the veil withdrawn
  'Twixt the artist's soul and works had left them heirs
Of speechless thoughts which would not quail nor
      fawn,
  Of angers and contempts, of hope and love :
For not without a meaning did he place
  The princely Urbino on the seat above
With everlasting shadow on his face,
  While the slow dawns and twilights disapprove
The ashes of his long-extinguished race
  Which never more shall clog the feet of men.
I do believe, divinest Angelo,
  That winter-hour in Via Larga, when
They bade thee build a statue up in snow *
  And straight that marvel of thine art again
Dissolved beneath the sun's Italian glow,
  Thine eyes, dilated with the plastic passion,
Thawing too in drops of wounded manhood, since,
  To mock alike thine art and indignation,
Laughed at the palace-window the new prince,—
  (" Aha ! this genius needs for exaltation,

---

\* This mocking task was set by Pietro, the unworthy successor of
Lorenzo the Magnificent.

When all's said and howe'er the proud may wince,
    A little marble from our princely mines!")
I do believe that hour thou laughedst too
    For the whole sad world and for thy Florentines,
After those few tears, which were only few!
    That as, beneath the sun, the grand white lines
Of thy snow-statue trembled and withdrew,—
    The head, erect as Jove's, being palsied first,
The eyelids flattened, the full brow turned blank,
    The right-hand, raised but now as if it cursed,
Dropt, a mere snowball, (till the people sank
    Their voices, though a louder laughter burst
From the royal window)—thou couldst proudly thank
    God and the prince for promise and presage,
And laugh the laugh back, I think verily,
    Thine eyes being purged by tears of righteous rage
To read a wrong into a prophecy,
    And measure a true great man's heritage
Against a mere great-duke's posterity.
    I think thy soul said then, "I do not need
A princedom and its quarries, after all;
    For if I write, paint, carve a word, indeed,
On book or board or dust, on floor or wall,
    The same is kept of God who taketh heed
That not a letter of the meaning fall
    Or ere it touch and teach His world's deep heart,

Outlasting, therefore, all your lordships, sir!
  So keep your stone, beseech you, for your part,
To cover up your grave-place and refer
  The proper titles; *I* live by my art.
The thought I threw into this snow shall stir
  This gazing people when their gaze is done;
And the tradition of your act and mine,
  When all the snow is melted in the sun,
Shall gather up, for unborn men, a sign
  Of what is the true princedom,—ay, and none
Shall laugh that day, except the drunk with wine."

  Amen, great Angelo! the day's at hand.
If many laugh not on it, shall we weep?
  Much more we must not, let us understand.
Through rhymers sonneteering in their sleep
  And archaists mumbling dry bones up the land
And sketchers lauding ruined towns a-heap,—
  Through all that drowsy hum of voices smooth,
The hopeful bird mounts carolling from brake,
  The hopeful child, with leaps to catch his growth,
Sings open-eyed for liberty's sweet sake:
  And I, a singer also from my youth,
Prefer to sing with these who are awake,
  With birds, with babes, with men who will not fear
The baptism of the holy morning dew,

(And many of such wakers now are here,
Complete in their anointed manhood, who
  Will greatly dare and greatlier persevere,)
Than join those old thin voices with my new,
  And sigh for Italy with some safe sigh
Cooped up in music 'twixt an oh and ah,—
  Nay, hand in hand with that young child, will I
Go singing rather, "*Bella libertà*,"
  Than, with those poets, croon the dead or cry
"*Se tu men bella fossi, Italia!*"

"Less wretched if less fair." Perhaps a truth
Is so far plain in this, that Italy,
  Long trammelled with the purple of her youth
Against her age's ripe activity,
  Sits still upon her tombs, without death's ruth
But also without life's brave energy.
  "Now tell us what is Italy?" men ask:
And others answer, "Virgil, Cicero,
  Catullus, Cæsar." What beside? to task
The memory closer—"Why, Boccaccio,
  Dante, Petrarca,"—and if still the flask
Appears to yield its wine by drops too slow,—
  "Angelo, Raffael, Pergolese,"—all
Whose strong hearts beat through stone, or charged
        again

The paints with fire of souls electrical,
Or broke up heaven for music. What more then?
Why, then, no more. The chaplet's last beads fall
In naming the last saintship within ken,
And, after that, none prayeth in the land.
Alas, this Italy has too long swept
Heroic ashes up for hour-glass sand;
Of her own past, impassioned nympholept!
Consenting to be nailed here by the hand
To the very bay-tree under which she stept
A queen of old, and plucked a leafy branch;
And, licensing the world too long indeed
To use her broad phylacteries to staunch
And stop her bloody lips, she takes no heed
How one clear word would draw an avalanche
Of living sons around her, to succeed
The vanished generations. Can she count
These oil-eaters with large live mobile mouths
Agape for macaroni, in the amount
Of consecrated heroes of her south's
Bright rosary? The pitcher at the fount,
The gift of gods, being broken, she much loathes
To let the ground-leaves of the place confer
A natural bowl. So henceforth she would seem
No nation, but the poet's pensioner,
With alms from every land of song and dream,

While aye her pipers sadly pipe of her
Until their proper breaths, in that extreme
   Of sighing, split the reed on which they played :
Of which, no more. But never say "no more"
   To Italy's life! Her memories undismayed
Still argue "evermore ;" her graves implore
   Her future to be strong and not afraid ;
Her very statues send their looks before.

We do not serve the dead—the past is past.
God lives, and lifts His glorious mornings up
   Before the eyes of men awake at last,
Who put away the meats they used to sup,
   And down upon the dust of earth outcast
The dregs remaining of the ancient cup,
   Then turn to wakeful prayer and worthy act.
The Dead, upon their awful 'vantage ground,
   The sun not in their faces, shall abstract
No more our strength ; we will not be discrowned
   As guardians of their crowns, nor deign transact
A barter of the present, for a sound
   Of good so counted in the foregone days.
O Dead, ye shall no longer cling to us
   With rigid hands of desiccating praise,
And drag us backward by the garment thus,
   To stand and laud you in long-drawn virelays !

We will not henceforth be oblivious
   Of our own lives, because ye lived before,
Nor of our acts, because ye acted well.
   We thank you that ye first unlatched the door,
But will not make it inaccessible
   By thankings on the threshold any more.
We hurry onward to extinguish hell
   With our fresh souls, our younger hope, and
      God's
Maturity of purpose.   Soon shall we
   Die also! and, that then our periods
Of life may round themselves to memory
   As smoothly as on our graves the burial-sods,
We now must look to it to excel as ye,
   And bear our age as far, unlimited
By the last mind-mark; so, to be invoked
   By future generations, as their Dead.

'T is true that when the dust of death has choked
   A great man's voice, the common words he said
Turn oracles, the common thoughts he yoked
   Like horses, draw like griffins: this is true
And acceptable.   I, too, should desire,
   When men make record, with the flowers they
      strew,
"Savonarola's soul went out in fire

Upon our Grand-duke's piazza,* and burned through
A moment first, or ere he did expire,
  The veil betwixt the right and wrong, and showed
How near God sat and judged the judges there,—"
  Upon the self-same pavement overstrewed
To cast my violets with as reverent care,
  And prove that all the winters which have snowed
Cannot snow out the scent from stones and air,
  Of a sincere man's virtues.  This was he,
Savonarola, who, while Peter sank
  With his whole boat-load, called courageously
"Wake Christ, wake Christ!"—who, having tried the tank
  Of old church-waters used for baptistry
Ere Luther came to spill them, swore they stank;
  Who also by a princely deathbed cried,
"Loose Florence, or God will not loose thy soul!"
  Then fell back the Magnificent and died
Beneath the star-look shooting from the cowl,
  Which turned to wormwood-bitterness the wide
Deep sea of his ambitions.  It were foul
  To grudge Savonarola and the rest
Their violets: rather pay them quick and fresh!

---

\* Savonarola was burnt for his testimony against papal corruptions as early as March, 1498: and, as late as our own day, it has been a custom in Florence to strew with violets the pavement where he suffered, in grateful recognition of the anniversary.

The emphasis of death makes manifest
The eloquence of action in our flesh;
  And men who, living, were but dimly guessed,
When once free from their life's entangled mesh,
  Show their full length in graves, or oft indeed
Exaggerate their stature, in the flat,
  To noble admirations which exceed
Most nobly, yet will calculate in that
  But accurately. We, who are the seed
Of buried creatures, if we turned and spat
  Upon our antecedents, we were vile.
Bring violets rather. If these had not walked
  Their furlong, could we hope to walk our mile?
Therefore bring violets. Yet if we self-baulked
  Stand still, a-strewing violets all the while,
These moved in vain, of whom we have vainly talked.
  So rise up henceforth with a cheerful smile,
And having strewn the violets, reap the corn,
  And having reaped and garnered, bring the plough
And draw new furrows 'neath the healthy morn,
  And plant the great Hereafter in this Now.

Of old 't was so. How step by step was worn,
  As each man gained on each securely!—how
Each by his own strength sought his own Ideal,—
  The ultimate Perfection leaning bright

From out the sun and stars to bless the leal
　　And earnest search of all for Fair and Right
Through doubtful forms by earth accounted real!
　　Because old Jubal blew into delight
The souls of men with clear-piped melodies,
　　If youthful Asaph were content at most
To draw from Jubal's grave, with listening eyes,
　　Traditionary music's floating ghost
Into the grass-grown silence, were it wise?
　　And was 't not wiser, Jubal's breath being lost,
That Miriam clashed her cymbals to surprise
　　The sun between her white arms flung apart,
With new glad golden sounds? that David's strings
　　O'erflowed his hand with music from his heart?
So harmony grows full from many springs,
　　And happy accident turns holy art.

You enter, in your Florence wanderings,
　　The church of Saint Maria Novella.　Pass
The left stair, where at plague-time Machiavel*
　　Saw One with set fair face as in a glass,
Dressed out against the fear of death and hell,
　　Rustling her silks in pauses of the mass,
To keep the thought off how her husband fell,
　　When she left home, stark dead across her feet,—

* See his description of the plague in Florence.

The stair leads up to what the Orgagnas save
  Of Dante's dæmons; you, in passing it,
Ascend the right stair from the farther nave
  To muse in a small chapel scarcely lit
By Cimabue's Virgin. Bright and brave,
  That picture was accounted, mark, of old:
A king stood bare before its sovran grace,*
  A reverent people shouted to behold
The picture, not the king, and even the place
  Containing such a miracle grew bold,
Named the Glad Borgo from that beauteous face
  Which thrilled the artist, after work, to think
His own ideal Mary-smile should stand
  So very near him,—he, within the brink
Of all that glory, let in by his hand
  With too divine a rashness! Yet none shrink
Who come to gaze here now; albeit 't was planned
  Sublimely in the thought's simplicity:
The Lady, throned in empyreal state,
  Minds only the young Babe upon her knee,
While sidelong angels bear the royal weight,

---

* Charles of Anjou, in his passage through Florence, was permitted to see this picture while yet in Cimabue's "bottega." The populace followed the royal visitor, and, from the universal delight and admiration, the quarter of the city in which the artist lived was called "Borgo Allegri." The picture was carried in triumph to the church, and deposited there.

Prostrated meekly, smiling tenderly
Oblivion of their wings; the Child thereat
   Stretching its hand like God.   If any should,
Because of some stiff draperies and loose joints,
   Gaze scorn down from the heights of Raffaelhood
On Cimabue's picture,—Heaven anoints
   The head of no such critic, and his blood
The poet's curse strikes full on and appoints
   To ague and cold spasms for evermore.
A noble picture! worthy of the shout
   Wherewith along the streets the people bore
Its cherub-faces which the sun threw out
   Until they stooped and entered the church door.
Yet rightly was young Giotto talked about,
   Whom Cimabue found among the sheep,*
And knew, as gods know gods, and carried home
   To paint the things he had painted, with a deep
And fuller insight, and so overcome
   His chapel-Lady with a heavenlier sweep
Of light: for thus we mount into the sum
   Of great things known or acted.   I hold, too,
That Cimabue smiled upon the lad

---

\* How Cimabue found Giotto, the shepherd-boy, sketching a ram of his flock upon a stone, is prettily told by Vasari,—who also relates that the elder artist Margheritone died "infastidito" of the successes of the new school.

At the first stroke which passed what he could do,
Or else his Virgin's smile had never had
   Such sweetness in 't.  All great men who foreknew
Their heirs in art, for art's sake have been glad,
   And bent their old white heads as if uncrowned,
Fanatics of their pure Ideals still
   Far more than of their triumphs, which were found
With some less vehement struggle of the will.
   If old Margheritone trembled, swooned
And died despairing at the open sill
   Of other men's achievements (who achieved,
By loving art beyond the master), he
   Was old Margheritone, and conceived
Never, at first youth and most ecstasy,
   A Virgin like that dream of one, which heaved
The death-sigh from his heart.  If wistfully
   Margheritone sickened at the smell
Of Cimabue's laurel, let him go !
   For Cimabue stood up very well
In spite of Giotto's, and Angelico
   The artist-saint kept smiling in his cell
The smile with which he welcomed the sweet slow
   Inbreak of angels (whitening through the dim
That he might paint them), while the sudden sense
   Of Raffael's future was revealed to him
By force of his own fair works' competence.

The same blue waters where the dolphins swim
Suggest the tritons. Through the blue Immense
　Strike out, all-swimmers! cling not in the way
Of one another, so to sink; but learn
　The strong man's impulse, catch the freshening
　　　spray
He throws up in his motions, and discern
　By his clear westering eye, the time of day.
Thou, God, hast set us worthy gifts to earn
　Besides Thy heaven and Thee! and when I say
There's room here for the weakest man alive
　To live and die, there's room too, I repeat,
For all the strongest to live well, and strive
　Their own way, by their individual heat,—
Like some new bee-swarm leaving the old hive,
　Despite the wax which tempts so violet-sweet.
Then let the living live, the dead retain
　Their grave-cold flowers!—though honour's best
　　　supplied
By bringing actions, to prove theirs not vain.

　Cold graves, we say? it shall be testified
That living men who burn in heart and brain,
　Without the dead were colder. If we tried
To sink the past beneath our feet, be sure
　The future would not stand. Precipitate

This old roof from the shrine, and, insecure,
  The nesting swallows fly off, mate from mate.
How scant the gardens, if the graves were fewer!
  The tall green poplars grew no longer straight
Whose tops not looked to Troy. Would any fight
  For Athens, and not swear by Marathon?
Who dared build temples, without tombs in sight?
  Or live, without some dead man's benison?
Or seek truth, hope for good, and strive for right,
  If, looking up, he saw not in the sun
Some angel of the martyrs all day long
  Standing and waiting? Your last rhythm will need
Your earliest key-note. Could I sing this song,
  If my dead masters had not taken heed
To help the heavens and earth to make me strong,
  As the wind ever will find out some reed
And touch it to such issues as belong
  To such a frail thing? None may grudge the Dead
Libations from full cups. Unless we choose
  To look back to the hills behind us spread,
The plains before us sadden and confuse;
  If orphaned, we are disinherited.

I would but turn these lachrymals to use,
  And pour fresh oil in from the olive-grove,
To furnish them as new lamps. Shall I say

What made my heart beat with exulting love
  A few weeks back?—
              The day was such a day
  As Florence owes the sun. The sky above,
Its weight upon the mountains seemed to lay,
  And palpitate in glory, like a dove
Who has flown too fast, full-hearted—take away
  The image! for the heart of man beat higher
That day in Florence, flooding all her streets
  And piazzas with a tumult and desire.
The people, with accumulated heats
  And faces turned one way, as if one fire
Both drew and flushed them, left their ancient beats
  And went up toward the palace-Pitti wall
To thank their Grand-duke who, not quite of course,
  Had graciously permitted, at their call,
The citizens to use their civic force
  To guard their civic homes. So, one and all,
The Tuscan cities streamed up to the source
  Of this new good at Florence, taking it
As good so far, presageful of more good,—
  The first torch of Italian freedom, lit
To toss in the next tiger's face who should
  Approach too near them in a greedy fit,—
The first pulse of an even flow of blood
  To prove the level of Italian veins

Towards rights perceived and granted. How we gazed
   From Casa Guidi windows while, in trains
Of orderly procession—banners raised,
   And intermittent bursts of martial strains
Which died upon the shout, as if amazed
   By gladness beyond music—they passed on!
The Magistracy, with insignia, passed,—
   And all the people shouted in the sun,
And all the thousand windows which had cast
   A ripple of silks in blue and scarlet down
(As if the houses overflowed at last),
   Seemed growing larger with fair heads and eyes.
The Lawyers passed,—and still arose the shout,
   And hands broke from the windows to surprise
Those grave calm brows with bay-tree leaves thrown out.
   The Priesthood passed,—the friars with worldly-wise
Keen sidelong glances from their beards about
   The street to see who shouted; many a monk
Who takes a long rope in the waist, was there:
   Whereat the popular exultation drunk
With indrawn "vivas" the whole sunny air,
   While through the murmuring windows rose and sunk
A cloud of kerchiefed hands,—"The church makes fair
   Her welcome in the new Pope's name." Ensued
The black sign of the "Martyrs"—(name no name,
   But count the graves in silence). Next were viewed

The Artists; next, the Trades; and after came
　　The People,—flag and sign, and rights as good—
And very loud the shout was for that same
　　Motto, "Il popolo." IL POPOLO,—
The word means dukedom, empire, majesty,
　　And kings in such an hour might read it so.
And next, with banners, each in his degree,
　　Deputed representatives a-row
Of every separate state of Tuscany:
　　Siena's she-wolf, bristling on the fold
Of the first flag, preceded Pisa's hare,
　　And Massa's lion floated calm in gold,
Pienza's following with his silver stare,
　　Arezzo's steed pranced clear from bridle-hold,—
And well might shout our Florence, greeting there
　　These, and more brethren. Last, the world had sent
The various children of her teeming flanks—
　　Greeks, English, French—as if to a parliament
Of lovers of her Italy in ranks,
　　Each bearing its land's symbol reverent;
At which the stones seemed breaking into thanks
　　And rattling up the sky, such sounds in proof
Arose; the very house-walls seemed to bend;
　　The very windows, up from door to roof,
Flashed out a rapture of bright heads, to mend
　　With passionate looks the gesture's whirling off

A hurricane of leaves.   Three hours did end
    While all these passed; and ever in the crowd,
Rude men, unconscious of the tears that kept
    Their beards moist, shouted; some few laughed aloud,
And none asked any why they laughed and wept:
    Friends kissed each other's cheeks, and foes long vowed
More warmly did it; two-months' babies leapt
    Right upward in their mother's arms, whose black
Wide glittering eyes looked elsewhere; lovers pressed
    Each before either, neither glancing back;
And peasant maidens smoothly 'tired and tressed
    Forgot to finger on their throats the slack
Great pearl-strings; while old blind men would not rest,
    But pattered with their staves and slid their shoes
Along the stones, and smiled as if they saw.
    O heaven, I think that day had noble use
Among God's days!   So near stood Right and Law,
    Both mutually forborne!   Law would not bruise
Nor Right deny, and each in reverent awe
    Honoured the other.   And if, ne'ertheless,
That good day's sun delivered to the vines
    No charta, and the liberal Duke's excess
Did scarce exceed a Guelf's or Ghibelline's
    In any special actual righteousness
Of what that day he granted, still the signs
    Are good and full of promise, we must say,

When multitudes approach their kings with prayers
    And kings concede their people's right to pray
Both in one sunshine.  Griefs are not despairs,
    So uttered, nor can royal claims dismay
When men from humble homes and ducal chairs
    Hate wrong together.  It was well to view
Those banners ruffled in a ruler's face
    Inscribed, "Live freedom, union, and all true
Brave patriots who are aided by God's grace!"
    Nor was it ill when Leopoldo drew
His little children to the window-place
    He stood in at the Pitti, to suggest
*They* too should govern as the people willed.
    What a cry rose then! some, who saw the best,
Declared his eyes filled up and overfilled
    With good warm human tears which unrepressed
Ran down.  I like his face; the forehead's build
    Has no capacious genius, yet perhaps
Sufficient comprehension,—mild and sad,
    And careful nobly,—not with care that wraps
Self-loving hearts, to stifle and make mad,
    But careful with the care that shuns a lapse
Of faith and duty, studious not to add
    A burden in the gathering of a gain.
And so, God save the Duke, I say with those
    Who that day shouted it; and while dukes reign,

May all wear in the visible overflows
  Of spirit, such a look of careful pain!
For God must love it better than repose.

And all the people who went up to let
  Their hearts out to that Duke, as has been told—
Where guess ye that the living people met,
  Kept tryst, formed ranks, chose leaders, first unrolled
Their banners?
                In the Loggia? where is set
  Cellini's godlike Perseus, bronze or gold,
(How name the metal, when the statue flings
  Its soul so in your eyes?) with brow and sword
Superbly calm, as all opposing things,
  Slain with the Gorgon, were no more abhorred
Since ended?
              No, the people sought no wings
  From Perseus in the Loggia, nor implored
An inspiration in the place beside
  From that dim bust of Brutus, jagged and grand,
Where Buonarroti passionately tried
  From out the close-clenched marble to demand
The head of Rome's sublimest homicide,
  Then dropt the quivering mallet from his hand,
Despairing he could find no model-stuff
  Of Brutus in all Florence where he found

The gods and gladiators thick enough.
   Nor there! the people chose still holier ground:
The people, who are simple, blind and rough,
   Know their own angels, after looking round.
Whom chose they then? where met they?

                              On the stone
   Called Dante's,—a plain flat stone scarce discerned
From others in the pavement,—whereupon
   He used to bring his quiet chair out, turned
To Brunelleschi's church, and pour alone
   The lava of his spirit when it burned:
It is not cold to-day. O passionate
   Poor Dante who, a banished Florentine,
Didst sit austere at banquets of the great
   And muse upon this far-off stone of thine
And think how oft some passer used to wait
   A moment, in the golden day's decline,
With "Good night, dearest Dante!"—well, good night!
   *I* muse now, Dante, and think verily,
Though chapelled in the byeway out of sight,
   Ravenna's bones would thrill with ecstasy,
Couldst know thy favourite stone's elected right
   As tryst-place for thy Tuscans to foresee
Their earliest chartas from. Good night, good morn,
   Henceforward, Dante! now my soul is sure

That thine is better comforted of scorn,
    And looks down earthward in completer cure
Than when, in Santa Croce church forlorn
    Of any corpse, the architect and hewer
Did pile the empty marbles as thy tomb.*
    For now thou art no longer exiled, now
Best honoured: we salute thee who art come
    Back to the old stone with a softer brow
Than Giotto drew upon the wall, for some
    Good lovers of our age to track and plough†
Their way to, through time's ordures stratified,
    And startle broad awake into the dull
Bargello chamber: now thou 'rt milder-eyed,—
    Now Beatrix may leap up glad to cull
Thy first smile, even in heaven and at her side,
    Like that which, nine years old, looked beautiful
At May-game. What do I say? I only meant
    That tender Dante loved his Florence well,
While Florence, now, to love him is content;
    And, mark ye, that the piercingest sweet smell
Of love's dear incense by the living sent

---

\* The Florentines, to whom the Ravennese refused the body of Dante (demanded of them "in a late remorse of love"), have given a cenotaph in this church to their divine poet. Something less than a grave!

† In allusion to Mr. Kirkup's discovery of Giotto's fresco portrait of Dante.

To find the dead, is not accessible
To lazy livers—no narcotic,—not
   Swung in a censer to a sleepy tune,—
But trod out in the morning air by hot
   Quick spirits who tread firm to ends foreshown,
And use the name of greatness unforgot,
   To meditate what greatness may be done.

For Dante sits in heaven and ye stand here,
   And more remains for doing, all must feel,
Than trysting on his stone from year to year
   To shift processions, civic toe to heel,
The town's thanks to the Pitti.  Are ye freer
   For what was felt that day? a chariot-wheel
May spin fast, yet the chariot never roll.
   But if that day suggested something good,
And bettered, with one purpose, soul by soul,—
   Better means freer.  A land's brotherhood
Is most puissant: men, upon the whole,
   Are what they can be,—nations, what they would.

Will therefore, to be strong, thou Italy!
   Will to be noble!  Austrian Metternich
Can fix no yoke unless the neck agree;
   And thine is like the lion's when the thick
Dews shudder from it, and no man would be

The stroker of his mane, much less would prick
His nostril with a reed.  When nations roar
   Like lions, who shall tame them and defraud
Of the due pasture by the river-shore?
   Roar, therefore! shake your dewlaps dry abroad:
The amphitheatre with open door
   Leads back upon the benches who applaud
The last spear-thruster.

                              Yet the Heavens forbid
   That we should call on passion to confront
The brutal with the brutal and, amid
   This ripening world, suggest a lion-hunt
And lion's-vengeance for the wrongs men did
   And do now, though the spears are getting blunt.
We only call, because the sight and proof
   Of lion-strength hurts nothing; and to show
A lion-heart, and measure paw with hoof,
   Helps something, even, and will instruct a foe
As well as the onslaught, how to stand aloof:
   Or else the world gets past the mere brute blow
Or given or taken.  Children use the fist
   Until they are of age to use the brain;
And so we needed Cæsars to assist
   Man's justice, and Napoleons to explain
God's counsel, when a point was nearly missed,

Until our generations should attain
Christ's stature nearer.   Not that we, alas,
  Attain already; but a single inch
Will raise to look down on the swordsman's pass.
  As knightly Roland on the coward's flinch:
And, after chloroform and ether-gas,
  We find out slowly what the bee and finch
Have ready found, through Nature's lamp in each,
  How to our races we may justify
Our individual claims and, as we reach
  Our own grapes, bend the top vines to supply
The children's uses,—how to fill a breach
  With olive-branches,—how to quench a lie
With truth, and smite a foe upon the cheek
  With Christ's most conquering kiss.   Why, these
        are things
Worth a great nation's finding, to prove weak
  The "glorious arms" of military kings.
And so with wide embrace, my England, seek
  To stifle the bad heat and flickerings
Of this world's false and nearly expended fire!
  Draw palpitating arrows to the wood,
And twang abroad thy high hopes and thy higher
  Resolves, from that most virtuous altitude!
Till nations shall unconsciously aspire
  By looking up to thee, and learn that good

And glory are not different.   Announce law
  By freedom; exalt chivalry by peace;
Instruct how clear calm eyes can overawe,
  And how pure hands, stretched simply to release
A bond-slave, will not need a sword to draw
  To be held dreadful.  O my England, crease
Thy purple with no alien agonies,
  No struggles toward encroachment, no vile war!
Disband thy captains, change thy victories,
  Be henceforth prosperous as the angels are,
Helping, not humbling.

                                Drums and battle-cries
  Go out in music of the morning-star—
And soon we shall have thinkers in the place
  Of fighters, each found able as a man
To strike electric influence through a race,
  Unstayed by city-wall and barbican.
The poet shall look grander in the face
  Than even of old (when he of Greece began
To sing "that Achillean wrath which slew
  So many heroes ")—seeing he shall treat
The deeds of souls heroic toward the true,
  The oracles of life, previsions sweet
And awful like divine swans gliding through
  White arms of Ledas, which will leave the heat

Of their escaping godship to endue
    The human medium with a heavenly flush.

Meanwhile, in this same Italy we want
    Not popular passion, to arise and crush,
But popular conscience, which may covenant
    For what it knows. Concede without a blush,
To grant the "civic guard" is not to grant
    The civic spirit, living and awake:
Those lappets on your shoulders, citizens,
    Your eyes strain after sideways till they ache
(While still, in admirations and amens,
    The crowd comes up on festa-days to take
The great sight in)—are not intelligence,
    Not courage even—alas, if not the sign
Of something very noble, they are nought;
    For every day ye dress your sallow kine
With fringes down their cheeks, though unbesought
    They loll their heavy heads and drag the wine
And bear the wooden yoke as they were taught
    The first day. What ye want is light—indeed
Not sunlight—(ye may well look up surprised
    To those unfathomable heavens that feed
Your purple hills)—but God's light organized
    In some high soul, crowned capable to lead
The conscious people, conscious and advised,—

For if we lift a people like mere clay,
It falls the same.   We want thee, O unfound
   And sovran teacher! if thy beard be grey
Or black, we bid thee rise up from the ground
   And speak the word God giveth thee to say,
Inspiring into all this people round,
   Instead of passion, thought, which pioneers
All generous passion, purifies from sin,
   And strikes the hour for.   Rise up, teacher! here's
A crowd to make a nation!—best begin
   By making each a man, till all be peers
Of earth's true patriots and pure martyrs in
   Knowing and daring.   Best unbar the doors
Which Peter's heirs keep locked so overclose
   They only let the mice across the floors,
While every churchman dangles, as he goes,
   The great key at his girdle, and abhors
In Christ's name, meekly.   Open wide the house,
   Concede the entrance with Christ's liberal mind,
And set the tables with His wine and bread.
   What! "commune in both kinds?" In every kind—
Wine, wafer, love, hope, truth, unlimited,
   Nothing kept back.   For when a man is blind
To starlight, will he see the rose is red?
   A bondsman shivering at a Jesuit's foot—
"Væ! meâ culpâ!"—is not like to stand

A freedman at a despot's and dispute
His titles by the balance in his hand,
  Weighing them "suo jure." Tend the root
If careful of the branches, and expand
  The inner souls of men before you strive
For civic heroes.

                But the teacher, where?
From all these crowded faces, all alive,
Eyes, of their own lids flashing themselves bare,
  And brows that with a mobile life contrive
A deeper shadow,—may we in no wise dare
  To put a finger out and touch a man,
And cry "this is the leader"? What, all these!
  Broad heads, black eyes,—yet not a soul that ran
From God down with a message? All, to please
  The donna waving measures with her fan,
And not the judgment-angel on his knees
  (The trumpet just an inch off from his lips),
Who when he breathes next, will put out the sun?

Yet mankind's self were foundered in eclipse,
If lacking doers, with great works to be done;
  And lo, the startled earth already dips
Back into light; a better day's begun;
  And soon this leader, teacher, will stand plain,

And build the golden pipes and synthesize
   This people-organ for a holy strain.
We hold this hope, and still in all these eyes
   Go sounding for the deep look which shall drain
Suffused thought into channelled enterprise.
   Where is the teacher? What now may he do,
Who shall do greatly? Doth he gird his waist
   With a monk's rope, like Luther? or pursue
The goat, like Tell? or dry his nets in haste,
   Like Masaniello when the sky was blue?
Keep house, like other peasants, with inlaced
   Bare brawny arms about a favourite child,
And meditative looks beyond the door
   (But not to mark the kidling's teeth have filed
The green shoots of his vine which last year bore
   Full twenty bunches), or, on triple-piled
Throne-velvets sit at ease to bless the poor,
   Like other pontiffs, in the Poorest's name?
The old tiara keeps itself aslope
   Upon his steady brows which, all the same,
Bend mildly to permit the people's hope?

   Whatever hand shall grasp this oriflamme,
Whatever man (last peasant or first pope
   Seeking to free his country) shall appear,
Teach, lead, strike fire into the masses, fill

These empty bladders with fine air, insphere
These wills into a unity of will,
  And make of Italy a nation—dear
And blessed be that man! the Heavens shall kill
  No leaf the earth lets grow for him, and Death
Shall cast him back upon the lap of Life
  To live more surely, in a clarion-breath
Of hero-music. Brutus with the knife,
  Rienzi with the fasces, throb beneath
Rome's stones,—and more who threw away joy's fife
  Like Pallas, that the beauty of their souls
Might ever shine untroubled and entire:
  But if it can be true that he who rolls
The Church's thunders will reserve her fire
  For only light,—from eucharistic bowls
Will pour new life for nations that expire,
  And rend the scarlet of his papal vest
To gird the weak loins of his countrymen,—
  I hold that he surpasses all the rest
Of Romans, heroes, patriots; and that when
  He sat down on the throne, he dispossessed
The first graves of some glory. See again,
  This country-saving is a glorious thing:
And if a common man achieved it? well.
  Say, a rich man did? excellent. A king?
That grows sublime. A priest? improbable.

A pope? Ah, there we stop, and cannot bring
Our faith up to the leap, with history's bell
　So heavy round the neck of it—albeit
We fain would grant the possibility
　For *thy* sake, Pio Nono!

　　　　　　　　　　Stretch thy feet
In that case—I will kiss them reverently
　As any pilgrim to the papal seat:
And, such proved possible, thy throne to me
　Shall seem as holy a place as Pellico's
Venetian dungeon, or as Spielberg's grate
　At which the Lombard woman hung the rose
Of her sweet soul by its own dewy weight,
　To feel the dungeon round her sunshine close,
And pining so, died early, yet too late
　For what she suffered. Yea, I will not choose
Betwixt thy throne, Pope Pius, and the spot
　Marked red for ever, spite of rains and dews,
Where Two fell riddled by the Austrian's shot,
　The brothers Bandiera, who accuse,
With one same mother-voice and face (that what
　They speak may be invincible) the sins
Of earth's tormentors before God the just,
　Until the unconscious thunderbolt begins
To loosen in His grasp.

                        And yet we must
　Beware, and mark the natural kiths and kins
Of circumstance and office, and distrust
　The rich man reasoning in a poor man's hut,
The poet who neglects pure truth to prove
　Statistic fact, the child who leaves a rut
For a smoother road, the priest who vows his glove
　Exhales no grace, the prince who walks afoot,
The woman who has sworn she will not love,
　And this Ninth Pius in Seventh Gregory's chair,
With Andrea Doria's forehead!

                            Count what goes
　To making up a pope, before he wear
That triple crown.　We pass the world-wide throes
　Which went to make the popedom,—the despair
Of free men, good men, wise men; the dread shows
　Of women's faces, by the faggot's flash
Tossed out, to the minutest stir and throb
　O' the white lips, the least tremble of a lash,
To glut the red stare of a licensed mob;
　The short mad cries down oubliettes, and plash
So horribly far off; priests, trained to rob,
　And kings that, like encouraged nightmares, sat
On nations' hearts most heavily distressed
　With monstrous sights and apophthegms of fate—

We pass these things,—because "the times" are prest
   With necessary charges of the weight
Of all this sin, and "Calvin, for the rest,
   Made bold to burn Servetus. Ah, men err!"—
And so do *churches*! which is all we mean
   To bring to proof in any register
Of theological fat kine and lean:
   So drive them back into the pens! refer
Old sins (with pourpoint, "quotha" and "I ween")
   Entirely to the old times, the old times;
Nor ever ask why this preponderant
   Infallible pure Church could set her chimes
Most loudly then, just then,—most jubilant,
   Precisely then, when mankind stood in crimes
Full heart-deep, and Heaven's judgments were not scant.
   Inquire still less, what signifies a church
Of perfect inspiration and pure laws
   Who burns the first man with a brimstone-torch,
And grinds the second, bone by bone, because
   The times, forsooth, are used to rack and scorch!
What *is* a holy Church unless she awes
   The times down from their sins? Did Christ select
Such amiable times to come and teach
   Love to, and mercy? The whole world were wrecked
If every mere great man, who lives to reach
   A little leaf of popular respect,

Attained not simply by some special breach
   In the age's customs, by some precedence
In thought and act, which, having proved him higher
   Than those he lived with, proved his competence
In helping them to wonder and aspire.

   My words are guiltless of the bigot's sense;
My soul has fire to mingle with the fire
   Of all these souls, within or out of doors
Of Rome's church or another. I believe
   In one Priest, and one temple with its floors
Of shining jasper gloom'd at morn and eve
   By countless knees of earnest auditors,
And crystal walls too lucid to perceive,
   That none may take the measure of the place
And say "So far the porphyry, then, the flint—
   To this mark mercy goes, and there ends grace,"
Though still the permeable crystals hint
   At some white starry distance, bathed in space.
I feel how nature's ice-crusts keep the dint
   Of undersprings of silent Deity.
I hold the articulated gospels which
   Show Christ among us crucified on tree.
I love all who love truth, if poor or rich
   In what they have won of truth possessively.
No altars and no hands defiled with pitch

Shall scare me off, but I will pray and eat
With all these—taking leave to choose my ewers—
And say at last "Your visible churches cheat
Their inward types; and, if a church assures
Of standing without failure and defeat,
The same both fails and lies."

         To leave which lures
Of wider subject through past years,—behold,
We come back from the popedom to the pope,
To ponder what he *must* be, ere we are bold
For what he *may* be, with our heavy hope
To trust upon his soul. So, fold by fold,
Explore this mummy in the priestly cope,
Transmitted through the darks of time, to catch
The man within the wrappage, and discern
How he, an honest man, upon the watch
Full fifty years for what a man may learn,
Contrived to get just there; with what a snatch
Of old-world oboli he had to earn
The passage through; with what a drowsy sop,
To drench the busy barkings of his brain;
What ghosts of pale tradition, wreathed with hop
'Gainst wakeful thought, he had to entertain
For heavenly visions; and consent to stop
The clock at noon, and let the hour remain

(Without vain windings-up) inviolate
Against all chimings from the belfry.  Lo,
   From every given pope you must abate,
Albeit you love him, some things—good, you know—
   Which every given heretic you hate,
Assumes for his, as being plainly so.
   A pope must hold by popes a little,—yes,
By councils, from Nicæa up to Trent,—
   By hierocratic empire, more or less
Irresponsible to men,—he must resent
   Each man's particular conscience, and repress
Inquiry, meditation, argument,
   As tyrants faction.  Also, he must not
Love truth too dangerously, but prefer
   "The interests of the Church" (because a blot
Is better than a rent, in miniver)—
   Submit to see the people swallow hot
Husk-porridge, which his chartered churchmen stir
   Quoting the only true God's epigraph,
"Feed my lambs, Peter!"—must consent to sit
   Attesting with his pastoral ring and staff
To such a picture of our Lady, hit
   Off well by artist-angels (though not half
As fair as Giotto would have painted it)—
   To such a vial, where a dead man's blood
Runs yearly warm beneath a churchman's finger,—

To such a holy house of stone and wood,
Whereof a cloud of angels was the bringer
  From Bethlehem to Loreto. Were it good
For any pope on earth to be a flinger
  Of stones against these high-niched counterfeits?
Apostates only are iconoclasts.
  He dares not say, while this false thing abets
That true thing, "This is false." He keeps his fasts
  And prayers, as prayer and fast were silver frets
To change a note upon a string that lasts,
  And make a lie a virtue. Now, if he
Did more than this, higher hoped, and braver dared,
  I think he were a pope in jeopardy,
Or no pope rather, for his truth had barred
  The vaulting of his life,—and certainly,
If he do only this, mankind's regard
  Moves on from him at once, to seek some new
Teacher and leader. He is good and great
  According to the deeds a pope can do;
Most liberal, save those bonds; affectionate,
  As princes may be, and, as priests are, true;
But only the Ninth Pius after eight,
  When all's praised most. At best and hopefullest,
He's pope—we want a man! his heart beats warm,
  But, like the prince enchanted to the waist,
He sits in stone and hardens by a charm

Into the marble of his throne high-placed.
Mild benediction waves his saintly arm—
  So, good! but what we want's a perfect man,
Complete and all alive: half travertine
  Half suits our need, and ill subserves our plan.
Feet, knees, nerves, sinews, energies divine
  Were never yet too much for men who ran
In such hard ways as must be this of thine,
  Deliverer whom we seek, whoe'er thou art,
Pope, prince, or peasant! If, indeed, the first,
  The noblest, therefore! since the heroic heart
Within thee must be great enough to burst
  Those trammels buckling to the baser part
Thy saintly peers in Rome, who crossed and cursed
  With the same finger.

                      Come, appear, be found,
If pope or peasant, come! we hear the cock,
  The courtier of the mountains when first crowned
With golden dawn; and orient glories flock
  To meet the sun upon the highest ground.
Take voice and work! we wait to hear thee knock
  At some one of our Florentine nine gates,
On each of which was imaged a sublime
  Face of a Tuscan genius, which, for hate's
And love's sake, both, our Florence in her prime

Turned boldly on all comers to her states,
As heroes turned their shields in antique time
   Emblazoned with honourable acts.  And though
The gates are blank now of such images,
   And Petrarch looks no more from Nicolo
Toward dear Arezzo, 'twixt the acacia-trees,
   Nor Dante, from gate Gallo—still we know,
Despite the razing of the blazonries,
   Remains the consecration of the shield:
The dead heroic faces will start out
   On all these gates, if foes should take the field,
And blend sublimely, at the earliest shout,
   With living heroes who will scorn to yield
A hair's-breadth even, when, gazing round about,
   They find in what a glorious company
They fight the foes of Florence.  Who will grudge
   His one poor life, when that great man we see
Has given five hundred years, the world being judge,
   To help the glory of his Italy?
Who, born the fair side of the Alps, will budge,
   When Dante stays, when Ariosto stays,
When Petrarch stays for ever?  Ye bring swords,
   My Tuscans?  Ay, if wanted in this haze,
Bring swords: but first bring souls!—bring thoughts and words,
   Unrusted by a tear of yesterday's,

Yet awful by its wrong,—and cut these cords,
  And mow this green lush falseness to the roots,
And shut the mouth of hell below the swathe!
  And, if ye can bring songs too, let the lute's
Recoverable music softly bathe
  Some poet's hand, that, through all bursts and bruits
Of popular passion, all unripe and rathe
  Convictions of the popular intellect,
Ye may not lack a finger up the air,
  Annunciative, reproving, pure, erect,
To show which way your first Ideal bare
  The whiteness of its wings when (sorely pecked
By falcons on your wrists) it unaware
  Arose up overhead and out of sight.


Meanwhile, let all the far ends of the world
  Breathe back the deep breath of their old delight,
To swell the Italian banner just unfurled.
  Help, lands of Europe! for, if Austria fight,
The drums will bar your slumber. Had ye curled
  The laurel for your thousand artists' brows,
If these Italian hands had planted none?
  Can any sit down idle in the house
Nor hear appeals from Buonarroti's stone
  And Raffael's canvas, rousing and to rouse?
Where's Poussin's master? Gallic Avignon

Bred Laura, and Vaucluse's fount has stirred
The heart of France too strongly, as it lets
　Its little stream out (like a wizard's bird
Which bounds upon its emerald wing and wets
　The rocks on each side), that she should not gird
Her loins with Charlemagne's sword when foes beset
　The country of her Petrarch. Spain may well
Be minded how from Italy she caught,
　To mingle with her tinkling Moorish bell,
A fuller cadence and a subtler thought.
　And even the New World, the receptacle
Of freemen, may send glad men, as it ought,
　To greet Vespucci Amerigo's door.
While England claims, by trump of poetry,
　Verona, Venice, the Ravenna-shore,
And dearer holds John Milton's Fiesole
　Than Langland's Malvern with the stars in flower.

And Vallombrosa, we two went to see
　Last June, beloved companion,—where sublime
The mountains live in holy families,
　And the slow pinewoods ever climb and climb
Half up their breasts, just stagger as they seize
　Some grey crag, drop back with it many a time,
And struggle blindly down the precipice.
　The Vallombrosan brooks were strewn as thick

That June-day, knee-deep with dead beechen leaves,
    As Milton saw them ere his heart grew sick
And his eyes blind.  I think the monks and beeves
    Are all the same too: scarce have they changed the wick
On good Saint Gualbert's altar which receives
    The convent's pilgrims; and the pool in front
(Wherein the hill-stream trout are cast, to wait
    The beatific vision and the grunt
Used at refectory) keeps its weedy state,
    To baffle saintly abbots who would count
The fish across their breviary nor 'bate
    The measure of their steps.  O waterfalls
And forests! sound and silence! mountains bare
    That leap up peak by peak and catch the palls
Of purple and silver mist to rend and share
    With one another, at electric calls
Of life in the sunbeams,—till we cannot dare
    Fix your shapes, count your number! we must think
Your beauty and your glory helped to fill
    The cup of Milton's soul so to the brink,
He never more was thirsty when God's will
    Had shattered to his sense the last chain-link
By which he had drawn from Nature's visible
    The fresh well-water.  Satisfied by this,
He sang of Adam's paradise and smiled,
    Remembering Vallombrosa.  Therefore is

The place divine to English man and child,
  And pilgrims leave their souls here in a kiss.

For Italy 's the whole earth's treasury, piled
  With reveries of gentle ladies, flung
Aside, like ravelled silk, from life's worn stuff;
  With coins of scholars' fancy, which, being rung
On work-day counter, still sound silver-proof;
  In short, with all the dreams of dreamers young,
Before their heads have time for slipping off
  Hope's pillow to the ground.   How oft, indeed,
We 've sent our souls out from the rigid north,
  On bare white feet which would not print nor bleed,
To climb the Alpine passes and look forth,
  Where booming low the Lombard rivers lead
To gardens, vineyards, all a dream is worth,—
  Sights, thou and I, Love, have seen afterward
From Tuscan Bellosguardo, wide awake,\*
  When, standing on the actual blessed sward
Where Galileo stood at nights to take
  The vision of the stars, we have found it hard,
Gazing upon the earth and heaven, to make
  A choice of beauty.

---

\* Galileo's villa, close to Florence, is built on an eminence called Bellosguardo.

                    Therefore let us all
Refreshed in England or in other land,
   By visions, with their fountain-rise and fall,
Of this earth's darling,—we, who understand
   A little how the Tuscan musical
Vowels do round themselves as if they planned
   Eternities of separate sweetness,—we,
Who loved Sorrento vines in picture-book,
   Or ere in wine-cup we pledged faith or glee,—
Who loved Rome's wolf with demi-gods at suck,
   Or ere we loved truth's own divinity,—
Who loved, in brief, the classic hill and brook,
   And Ovid's dreaming tales and Petrarch's song,
Or ere we loved Love's self even,—let us give
   The blessing of our souls (and wish them strong
To bear it to the height where prayers arrive,
   When faithful spirits pray against a wrong,)
To this great cause of southern men who strive
   In God's name for man's rights, and shall not fail.

Behold, they shall not fail. The shouts ascend
   Above the shrieks, in Naples, and prevail.
Rows of shot corpses, waiting for the end
   Of burial, seem to smile up straight and pale
Into the azure air and apprehend
   That final gun-flash from Palermo's coast

Which lightens their apocalypse of death.
  So let them die! The world shows nothing lost;
Therefore, not blood. Above or underneath,
  What matter, brothers, if ye keep your post
On duty's side? As sword returns to sheath,
  So dust to grave, but souls find place in Heaven.
Heroic daring is the true success,
  The eucharistic bread requires no leaven;
And though your ends were hopeless, we should bless
  Your cause as holy. Strive—and, having striven,
Take, for God's recompense, that righteousness!

## PART II.

I WROTE a meditation and a dream,
    Hearing a little child sing in the street:
I leant upon his music as a theme,
    Till it gave way beneath my heart's full beat
Which tried at an exultant prophecy
    But dropped before the measure was complete—
Alas, for songs and hearts! O Tuscany,
    O Dante's Florence, is the type too plain?
Didst thou, too, only sing of liberty
    As little children take up a high strain
With unintentioned voices, and break off
    To sleep upon their mothers' knees again?
Couldst thou not watch one hour? then, sleep enough—
    That sleep may hasten manhood and sustain
The faint pale spirit with some muscular stuff.

But we, who cannot slumber as thou dost,
    We thinkers, who have thought for thee and failed,
    We hopers, who have hoped for thee and lost,

We poets, wandered round by dreams,* who hailed
   From this Atrides' roof (with lintel-post
Which still drips blood,—the worse part hath prevailed)
   The fire-voice of the beacons to declare
Troy taken, sorrow ended,—cozened through
   A crimson sunset in a misty air,
What now remains for such as we, to do?
   God's judgments, peradventure, will He bare
To the roots of thunder, if we kneel and sue?

From Casa Guidi windows I looked forth,
And saw ten thousand eyes of Florentines
   Flash back the triumph of the Lombard north,—
Saw fifty banners, freighted with the signs
   And exultations of the awakened earth,
Float on above the multitude in lines,
   Straight to the Pitti. So, the vision went.
And so, between those populous rough hands
   Raised in the sun, Duke Leopold outleant,
And took the patriot's oath which henceforth stands
   Among the oaths of perjurers, eminent
To catch the lightnings ripened for these lands.

Why swear at all, thou false Duke Leopold?
What need to swear? What need to boast thy blood

---

* See the opening passage of the "Agamemnon" of Æschylus.

Unspoilt of Austria, and thy heart unsold
Away from Florence? It was understood
   God made thee not too vigorous or too bold;
And men had patience with thy quiet mood,
   And women, pity, as they saw thee pace
Their festive streets with premature grey hairs.
   We turned the mild dejection of thy face
To princely meanings, took thy wrinkling cares
   For ruffling hopes, and called thee weak, not base.
Nay, better light the torches for more prayers
   And smoke the pale Madonnas at the shrine,
Being still "our poor Grand-duke, our good Grand-duke,
   Who cannot help the Austrian in his line,"—
Than write an oath upon a nation's book
   For men to spit at with scorn's blurring brine!
Who dares forgive what none can overlook?

   For me, I do repent me in this dust
Of towns and temples which makes Italy,—
   I sigh amid the sighs which breathe a gust
Of dying century to century
   Around us on the uneven crater-crust
Of these old worlds,—I bow my soul and knee.
   Absolve me, patriots, of my woman's fault
That ever I believed the man was true!
   These sceptred strangers shun the common salt,

And, therefore, when the general board's in view
   And they stand up to carve for blind and halt,
The wise suspect the viands which ensue.
   I much repent that, in this time and place
Where many corpse-lights of experience burn
   From Cæsar's and Lorenzo's festering race,
To enlighten groping reasoners, I could learn
   No better counsel for a simple case
Than to put faith in princes, in my turn.
   Had all the death-piles of the ancient years
Flared up in vain before me? knew I not
   What stench arises from some purple gears?
And how the sceptres witness whence they got
   Their briar-wood, crackling through the atmosphere's
Foul smoke, by princely perjuries, kept hot?
   Forgive me, ghosts of patriots,—Brutus, thou,
Who trailest downhill into life again
   Thy blood-weighed cloak, to indict me with thy slow
Reproachful eyes!—for being taught in vain
   That, while the illegitimate Cæsars show
Of meaner stature than the first full strain
   (Confessed incompetent to conquer Gaul),
They swoon as feebly and cross Rubicons
   As rashly as any Julius of them all!
Forgive, that I forgot the mind which runs
   Through absolute races, too unsceptical!

I saw the man among his little sons,
  His lips were warm with kisses while he swore;
And I, because I am a woman—I,
  Who felt my own child's coming life before
The prescience of my soul, and held faith high,—
  I could not bear to think, whoever bore,
That lips, so warmed, could shape so cold a lie.

From Casa Guidi windows I looked out,
Again looked, and beheld a different sight.
  The Duke had fled before the people's shout
"Long live the Duke!" A people, to speak right,
  Must speak as soft as courtiers, lest a doubt
Should curdle brows of gracious sovereigns, white.
  Moreover that same dangerous shouting meant
Some gratitude for future favours, which
  Were only promised, the Constituent
Implied, the whole being subject to the hitch
  In "motu proprios," very incident
To all these Czars, from Paul to Paulovitch.
  Whereat the people rose up in the dust
Of the ruler's flying feet, and shouted still
  And loudly; only, this time, as was just,
Not "Live the Duke," who had fled for good or ill,
  But "Live the People," who remained and must,
The unrenounced and unrenounceable.

Long live the people! How they lived! and boiled
And bubbled in the cauldron of the street:
  How the young blustered, nor the old recoiled,
And what a thunderous stir of tongues and feet
  Trod flat the palpitating bells and foiled
The joy-guns of their echo, shattering it!
  How down they pulled the Duke's arms every-
    where!
How up they set new café-signs, to show
  Where patriots might sip ices in pure air—
(The fresh paint smelling somewhat)! To and fro
  How marched the civic guard, and stopped to stare
When boys broke windows in a civic glow!
  How rebel songs were sung to loyal tunes,
And bishops cursed in ecclesiastic metres:
  How all the Circoli grew large as moons,
And all the speakers, moonstruck,—thankful greeters
  Of prospects which struck poor the ducal boons,
A mere free Press, and Chambers!—frank repeaters
  Of great Guerazzi's praises—"There's a man,
The father of the land, who, truly great,
  Takes off that national disgrace and ban,
The farthing tax upon our Florence-gate,
  And saves Italia as he only can!"
How all the nobles fled, and would not wait,
  Because they were most noble,—which being so,

How Liberals vowed to burn their palaces,
  Because free Tuscans were not free to go!
How grown men raged at Austria's wickedness,
  And smoked,—while fifty striplings in a row
Marched straight to Piedmont for the wrong's redress!
  You say we failed in duty, we who wore
Black velvet like Italian democrats,
  Who slashed our sleeves like patriots, nor forswore
The true republic in the form of hats?
  We chased the archbishop from the Duomo door,
We chalked the walls with bloody caveats
  Against all tyrants. If we did not fight
Exactly, we fired muskets up the air
  To show that victory was ours of right.
We met, had free discussion everywhere
  (Except perhaps i' the Chambers) day and night.
We proved the poor should be employed, . . . that's
    fair,—
  And yet the rich not worked for anywise,—
Pay certified, yet payers abrogated,—
  Full work secured, yet liabilities
To overwork excluded,—not one bated
  Of all our holidays, that still, at twice
Or thrice a week, are moderately rated.
  We proved that Austria was dislodged, or would
Or should be, and that Tuscany in arms

Should, would dislodge her, ending the old feud;
And yet, to leave our piazzas, shops, and farms,
 For the simple sake of fighting, was not good—
We proved that also. "Did we carry charms
 Against being killed ourselves, that we should rush
On killing others? what, desert herewith
 Our wives and mothers?—was that duty? tush!"
At which we shook the sword within the sheath
 Like heroes—only louder; and the flush
Ran up the cheek to meet the future wreath.
 Nay, what we proved, we shouted—how we shouted
(Especially the boys did), boldly planting
 That tree of liberty, whose fruit is doubted,
Because the roots are not of nature's granting!
 A tree of good and evil: none, without it,
Grow gods; alas and, with it, men are wanting!

 O holy knowledge, holy liberty,
O holy rights of nations! If I speak
 These bitter things against the jugglery
Of days that in your names proved blind and weak,
 It is that tears are bitter. When we see
The brown skulls grin at death in churchyards bleak,
 We do not cry "This Yorick is too light,"
For death grows deathlier with that mouth he makes.
 So with my mocking: bitter things I write

Because my soul is bitter for your sakes,
   O freedom! O my Florence!

                              Men who might
Do greatly in a universe that breaks
   And burns, must ever *know* before they do.
Courage and patience are but sacrifice;
   And sacrifice is offered for and to
Something conceived of. Each man pays a price
   For what himself counts precious, whether true
Or false the appreciation it implies.
   But here,—no knowledge, no conception, nought!
Desire was absent, that provides great deeds
   From out the greatness of prevenient thought:
And action, action, like a flame that needs
   A steady breath and fuel, being caught
Up, like a burning reed from other reeds,
   Flashed in the empty and uncertain air,
Then wavered, then went out. Behold, who blames
   A crooked course, when not a goal is there
To round the fervid striving of the games?
   An ignorance of means may minister
To greatness, but an ignorance of aims
   Makes it impossible to be great at all.
So with our Tuscans! Let none dare to say,
   " Here virtue never can be national;

Here fortitude can never cut a way
  Between the Austrian muskets, out of thrall:
I tell you rather that, whoever may
  Discern true ends here, shall grow pure enough
To love them, brave enough to strive for them,
  And strong to reach them though the roads be rough:
That having learnt—by no mere apophthegm—
  Not just the draping of a graceful stuff
About a statue, broidered at the hem,—
  Not just the trilling on an opera-stage
Of "libertà" to bravos—(a fair word,
  Yet too allied to inarticulate rage
And breathless sobs, for singing, though the chord
  Were deeper than they struck it) but the gauge
Of civil wants sustained and wrongs abhorred,
  The serious sacred meaning and full use
Of freedom for a nation,—then, indeed,
  Our Tuscans, underneath the bloody dews
Of some new morning, rising up agreed
  And bold, will want no Saxon souls or thews
To sweep their piazzas clear of Austria's breed.

  Alas, alas! it was not so this time.
Conviction was not, courage failed, and truth
  Was something to be doubted of. The mime
Changed masks, because a mime. The tide as smooth

In running in as out, no sense of crime
Because no sense of virtue,—sudden ruth
  Seized on the people: they would have again
Their good Grand-duke and leave Guerazzi, though
  He took that tax from Florence. "Much in vain
He takes it from the market-carts, we trow,
  While urgent that no market-men remain,
But all march off and leave the spade and plough,
  To die among the Lombards. Was it thus
The dear paternal Duke did? Live the Duke!"
  At which the joy-bells multitudinous,
Swept by an opposite wind, as loudly shook.
  Call back the mild archbishop to his house,
To bless the people with his frightened look,—
  He shall not yet be hanged, you comprehend!
Seize on Guerazzi; guard him in full view,
  Or else we stab him in the back, to end!
Rub out those chalked devices, set up new
  The Duke's arms, doff your Phrygian caps, and men
The pavement of the piazzas broke into
  By barren poles of freedom: smooth the way
For the ducal carriage, lest his highness sigh
  "Here trees of liberty grew yesterday!"
"Long live the Duke!"—how roared the cannonry,
  How rocked the bell-towers, and through thickening
    spray

Of nosegays, wreaths, and kerchiefs tossed on high,
   How marched the civic guard, the people still
Being good at shouts, especially the boys!
   Alas, poor people, of an unfledged will
Most fitly expressed by such a callow voice!
   Alas, still poorer Duke, incapable
Of being worthy even of so much noise!

   You think he came back instantly, with thanks
And tears in his faint eyes, and hands extended
   To stretch the franchise through their utmost ranks?
That having, like a father, apprehended,
   He came to pardon fatherly those pranks
Played out and now in filial service ended?—
   That some love-token, like a prince, he threw
To meet the people's love-call, in return?
   Well, how he came I will relate to you;
And if your hearts should burn, why, hearts *must* burn,
   To make the ashes which things old and new
Shall be washed clean in—as this Duke will learn.

   From Casa Guidi windows gazing, then,
I saw and witness how the Duke came back.
   The regular tramp of horse and tread of men
Did smite the silence like an anvil black
   And sparkless. With her wide eyes at full strain,

Our Tuscan nurse exclaimed "Alack, alack,
   Signora! these shall be the Austrians." "Nay,
Be still," I answered, "do not wake the child!"
   —For so, my two-months' baby sleeping lay
In milky dreams upon the bed and smiled,
   And I thought "He shall sleep on, while he may,
Through the world's baseness: not being yet defiled,
   Why should he be disturbed by what is done?"
Then, gazing, I beheld the long-drawn street
   Live out, from end to end, full in the sun,
With Austria's thousand; sword and bayonet,
   Horse, foot, artillery,—cannons rolling on
Like blind slow storm-clouds gestant with the heat
   Of undeveloped lightnings, each bestrode
By a single man, dust-white from head to heel,
   Indifferent as the dreadful thing he rode,
Like a sculptured Fate serene and terrible.
   As some smooth river which has overflowed
Will slow and silent down its current wheel
   A loosened forest, all the pines erect,
So swept, in mute significance of storm,
   The marshalled thousands; not an eye deflect
To left or right, to catch a novel form
   Of Florence city adorned by architect
And carver, or of Beauties live and warm
   Scared at the casements,—all, straightforward eyes

And faces, held as steadfast as their swords,
  And cognizant of acts, not imageries.
The key, O Tuscans, too well fits the wards!
  Ye asked for mimes,—these bring you tragedies:
For purple,—these shall wear it as your lords.
  Ye played like children,—die like innocents.
Ye mimicked lightnings with a torch,—the crack
  Of the actual bolt, your pastime circumvents.
Ye called up ghosts, believing they were slack
  To follow any voice from Gilboa's tents, . . .
Here's Samuel!—and, so, Grand-dukes come back!

And yet, they are no prophets though they come:
That awful mantle, they are drawing close,
  Shall be searched, one day, by the shafts of Doom
Through double folds now hoodwinking the brows.
  Resuscitated monarchs disentomb
Grave-reptiles with them, in their new life-throes.
  Let such beware.  Behold, the people waits,
Like God: as He, in His serene of might,
  So they, in their endurance of long straits.
Ye stamp no nation out, though day and night
  Ye tread them with that absolute heel which grates
And grinds them flat from all attempted height.
  You kill worms sooner with a garden-spade
Than you kill peoples: peoples will not die;

The tail curls stronger when you lop the head:
They writhe at every wound and multiply
  And shudder into a heap of life that's made
Thus vital from God's own vitality.
  'T is hard to shrivel back a day of God's
Once fixed for judgment; 't is as hard to change
  The peoples, when they rise beneath their loads
And heave them from their backs with violent wrench
  To crush the oppressor: for that judgment-rod's
The measure of this popular revenge.

  Meanwhile, from Casa Guidi windows, we
Beheld the armament of Austria flow
  Into the drowning heart of Tuscany:
And yet none wept, none cursed, or, if 't was so,
  They wept and cursed in silence. Silently
Our noisy Tuscans watched the invading foe;
  They had learnt silence. Pressed against the wall,
And grouped upon the church-steps opposite,
  A few pale men and women stared at all.
God knows what they were feeling, with their white
  Constrainèd faces, they, so prodigal
Of cry and gesture when the world goes right,
  Or wrong indeed. But here was depth of wrong,
And here, still water; they were silent here;
  And through that sentient silence, struck along

That measured tramp from which it stood out clear,
   Distinct the sound and silence, like a gong
At midnight, each by the other awfuller,—
   While every soldier in his cap displayed
A leaf of olive.  Dusty, bitter thing!
   Was such plucked at Novara, is it said?

A cry is up in England, which doth ring
   The hollow world through, that for ends of trade
And virtue and God's better worshipping,
   We henceforth should exalt the name of Peace
And leave those rusty wars that eat the soul,—
   Besides their clippings at our golden fleece.
I, too, have loved peace, and from bole to bole
   Of immemorial undeciduous trees
Would write, as lovers use upon a scroll,
   The holy name of Peace and set it high
Where none could pluck it down.  On trees, I say,—
   Not upon gibbets!—With the greenery
Of dewy branches and the flowery May,
   Sweet mediation betwixt earth and sky
Providing, for the shepherd's holiday.
   Not upon gibbets! though the vulture leaves
The bones to quiet, which he first picked bare.
   Not upon dungeons! though the wretch who grieves
And groans within less stirs the outer air

Than any little field-mouse stirs the sheaves.
Not upon chain-bolts! though the slave's despair
   Has dulled his helpless miserable brain
And left him blank beneath the freeman's whip
   To sing and laugh out idiocies of pain.
Nor yet on starving homes! where many a lip
   Has sobbed itself asleep through curses vain.
I love no peace which is not fellowship
   And which includes not mercy. I would have
Rather the raking of the guns across
   The world, and shrieks against Heaven's architrave;
Rather the struggle in the slippery fosse
   Of dying men and horses, and the wave
Blood-bubbling. . . . Enough said!—by Christ's own
      cross,
   And by this faint heart of my womanhood,
Such things are better than a Peace that sits
   Beside a hearth in self-commended mood,
And takes no thought how wind and rain by fits
   Are howling out of doors against the good
Of the poor wanderer. What! your peace admits
   Of outside anguish while it keeps at home?
I loathe to take its name upon my tongue.
   'T is nowise peace: 't is treason, stiff with doom,—
'T is gagged despair and inarticulate wrong,—
   Annihilated Poland, stifled Rome,

Dazed Naples, Hungary fainting 'neath the thong,
  And Austria wearing a smooth olive-leaf
On her brute forehead, while her hoofs outpress
  The life from these Italian souls, in brief.
O Lord of Peace, who art Lord of Righteousness,
  Constrain the anguished worlds from sin and grief,
Pierce them with conscience, purge them with redress,
  And give us peace which is no counterfeit!

But wherefore should we look out any more
  From Casa Guidi windows? Shut them straight,
And let us sit down by the folded door,
  And veil our saddened faces and, so, wait
What next the judgment-heavens make ready for.
  I have grown too weary of these windows. Sights
Come thick enough and clear enough in thought,
  Without the sunshine; souls have inner lights.
And since the Grand-duke has come back and brought
  This army of the North which thus requites
His filial South, we leave him to be taught.
  His South, too, has learnt something certainly,
Whereof the practice will bring profit soon;
  And peradventure other eyes may see,
From Casa Guidi windows, what is done
  Or undone. Whatsoever deeds they be,
Pope Pius will be glorified in none.

Record that gain, Mazzini!—it shall top
Some heights of sorrow. Peter's rock, so named,
Shall lure no vessel any more to drop
Among the breakers. Peter's chair is shamed
Like any vulgar throne the nations lop
To pieces for their firewood unreclaimed,—
And, when it burns too, we shall see as well
In Italy as elsewhere. Let it burn.
The cross, accounted still adorable,
Is Christ's cross only!—if the thief's would earn
Some stealthy genuflexions, we rebel;
And here the impenitent thief's has had its turn,
As God knows; and the people on their knees
Scoff and toss back the crosiers stretched like yokes
To press their heads down lower by degrees.
So Italy, by means of these last strokes,
Escapes the danger which preceded these,
Of leaving captured hands in cloven oaks,—
Of leaving very souls within the buckle
Whence bodies struggled outward,—of supposing
That freemen may like bondsmen kneel and truckle,
And then stand up as usual, without losing
An inch of stature.
                    Those whom she-wolves suckle
Will bite as wolves do in the grapple-closing
Of adverse interests. This at last is known

(Thank Pius for the lesson), that albeit
   Among the popedom's hundred heads of stone
Which blink down on you from the roof's retreat
   In Siena's tiger-striped cathedral, Joan
And Borgia 'mid their fellows you may greet,
   A harlot and a devil,—you will see
Not a man, still less angel, grandly set
   With open soul to render man more free.
The fishers are still thinking of the net,
   And, if not thinking of the hook too, we
Are counted somewhat deeply in their debt;
   But that's a rare case—so, by hook and crook
They take the advantage, agonizing Christ
   By rustier nails than those of Cedron's brook,
I' the people's body very cheaply priced,—
   And quote high priesthood out of Holy book,
While buying death-fields with the sacrificed.

   Priests, priests,—there's no such name!—God's
      own, except
Ye take most vainly. Through heaven's lifted gate
   The priestly ephod in sole glory swept
When Christ ascended, entered in, and sate
   (With victor face sublimely overwept)
At Deity's right hand, to mediate,
   He alone, He for ever. On His breast

The Urim and the Thummim, fed with fire
　　From the full Godhead, flicker with the unrest
Of human pitiful heart-beats. Come up higher,
　　All Christians! Levi's tribe is dispossest.
That solitary alb ye shall admire,
　　But not cast lots for. The last chrism, poured right,
Was on that Head, and poured for burial
　　And not for domination in men's sight.
What *are* these churches? The old temple-wall
　　Doth overlook them juggling with the sleight
Of surplice, candlestick and altar-pall;
　　East church and west church, ay, north church and
　　　　south,
Rome's church and England's,—let them all repent,
　　And make concordats 'twixt their soul and mouth,
Succeed Saint Paul by working at the tent,
　　Become infallible guides by speaking truth,
And excommunicate their pride that bent
　　And cramped the souls of men.
　　　　　　　　　　　　　Why, even here
Priestcraft burns out, the twinèd linen blazes;
　　Not, like asbestos, to grow white and clear,
But all to perish!—while the fire-smell raises
　　To life some swooning spirits who, last year,
Lost breath and heart in these church-stifled places.
　　Why, almost, through this Pius, we believed

The priesthood could be an honest thing, he smiled
  So saintly while our corn was being sheaved
For his own granaries! Showing now defiled
  His hireling hands, a better help 's achieved
Than if they blessed us shepherd-like and mild.
  False doctrine, strangled by its own amen,
Dies in the throat of all this nation. Who
  Will speak a pope's name as they rise again?
What woman or what child will count him true?
  What dreamer praise him with the voice or pen?
What man fight for him?—Pius takes his due.


  Record that gain, Mazzini!—Yes, but first
Set down thy people's faults; set down the want
  Of soul-conviction; set down aims dispersed,
And incoherent means, and valour scant
  Because of scanty faith, and schisms accursed
That wrench these brother-hearts from covenant
  With freedom and each other. Set down this,
And this, and see to overcome it when
  The seasons bring the fruits thou wilt not miss
If wary. Let no cry of patriot men
  Distract thee from the stern analysis
Of masses who cry only! keep thy ken
  Clear as thy soul is virtuous. Heroes' blood

Splashed up against thy noble brow in Rome;
   Let such not blind thee to an interlude
Which was not also holy, yet did come
   'Twixt sacramental actions,—brotherhood
Despised even there, and something of the doom
   Of Remus in the trenches. Listen now—
Rossi died silent near where Cæsar died.
   HE did not say "My Brutus, is it thou?"
But Italy unquestioned testified
   "*I* killed him! *I* am Brutus.—I avow."
At which the whole world's laugh of scorn replied
   "A poor maimed copy of Brutus!"
                                  Too much like,
Indeed, to be so unlike! too unskilled
   At Philippi and the honest battle-pike,
To be so skilful where a man is killed
   Near Pompey's statue, and the daggers strike
At unawares i' the throat. Was thus fulfilled
   An omen once of Michel Angelo?—
When Marcus Brutus he conceived complete,
   And strove to hurl him out by blow on blow
Upon the marble, at Art's thunderheat,
   Till haply (some pre-shadow rising slow
Of what his Italy would fancy meet
   To be called BRUTUS) straight his plastic hand
Fell back before his prophet-soul, and left

A fragment, a maimed Brutus,—but more grand
Than this, so named at Rome, was !

         Let thy weft
 Present one woof and warp, Mazzini! Stand
With no man hankering for a dagger's heft,
 No, not for Italy!—nor stand apart,
No, not for the Republic!—from those pure
 Brave men who hold the level of thy heart
In patriot truth, as lover and as doer,
 Albeit they will not follow where thou art
As extreme theorist. Trust and distrust fewer;
 And so bind strong and keep unstained the cause
Which (God's sign granted) war-trumps newly blown
 Shall yet annunciate to the world's applause.

But now, the world is busy; it has grown
 A Fair-going world. Imperial England draws
The flowing ends of the earth from Fez, Canton,
 Delhi and Stockholm, Athens and Madrid,
The Russias and the vast Americas,
 As if a queen drew in her robes amid
Her golden cincture,—isles, peninsulas,
 Capes, continents, far inland countries hid
By jasper-sands and hills of chrysopras,
 All trailing in their splendours through the door
Of the gorgeous Crystal Palace. Every nation,

To every other nation strange of yore,
Gives face to face the civic salutation,
   And holds up in a proud right hand before
That congress the best work which she can fashion
   By her best means. "These corals, will you please
To match against your oaks? They grow as fast
   Within my wilderness of purple seas."—
"This diamond stared upon me as I passed
   (As a live god's eye from a marble frieze)
Along a dark of diamonds. Is it classed?"—
   "I wove these stuffs so subtly that the gold
Swims to the surface of the silk like cream
   And curdles to fair patterns. Ye behold!"—
"These delicatest muslins rather seem
   Than be, you think? Nay, touch them and be bold,
Though such veiled Chakhi's face in Hafiz' dream."—
   "These carpets—you walk slow on them like kings,
Inaudible like spirits, while your foot
   Dips deep in velvet roses and such things."—
"Even Apollonius might commend this flute:*
   The music, winding through the stops, upsprings
To make the player very rich: compute!"

---

* Philostratus relates of Apollonius how he objected to the musical instrument of Linus the Rhodian that it could not enrich or beautify. The history of music in our day would satisfy the philosopher on one point at least.

"Here's goblet-glass, to take in with your wine
The very sun its grapes were ripened under:
   Drink light and juice together, and each fine."—
"This model of a steamship moves your wonder?
   You should behold it crushing down the brine
Like a blind Jove who feels his way with thunder."—
   "Here's sculpture! Ah, *we* live too! why not throw
Our life into our marbles? Art has place
   For other artists after Angelo."—
"I tried to paint out here a natural face;
   For nature includes Raffael, as we know,
Not Raffael nature. Will it help my case?"—
   "Methinks you will not match this steel of ours!"—
"Nor you this porcelain! One might dream the clay
   Retained in it the larvæ of the flowers,
They bud so, round the cup, the old Spring-way."—
   "Nor you these carven woods, where birds in bowers
With twisting snakes and climbing cupids, play."

   O Magi of the east and of the west,
Your incense, gold and myrrh are excellent!—
   What gifts for Christ, then, bring ye with the rest?
Your hands have worked well: is your courage spent
   In handwork only? Have you nothing best,
Which generous souls may perfect and present,
   And He shall thank the givers for? no light

Of teaching, liberal nations, for the poor
   Who sit in darkness when it is not night?
No cure for wicked children? Christ,—no cure!
   No help for women sobbing out of sight
Because men made the laws? no brothel-lure
   Burnt out by popular lightnings? Hast thou four
No remedy, my England, for such woes?
   No outlet, Austria, for the scourged and bound,
No entrance for the exiled? no repose,
   Russia, for knouted Poles worked underground,
And gentle ladies bleached among the snows?
   No mercy for the slave, America?
No hope for Rome, free France, chivalric France?
   Alas, great nations have great shames, I say.
No pity, O world, no tender utterance
   Of benediction, and prayers stretched this way
For poor Italia, baffled by mischance?
   O gracious nations, give some ear to me!
You all go to your Fair, and I am one
   Who at the roadside of humanity
Beseech your alms,—God's justice to be done.
   So, prosper!

            In the name of Italy,
Meantime, her patriot Dead have benison.
   They only have done well; and, what they did

Being perfect, it shall triumph. Let them slumber:
  No king of Egypt in a pyramid
Is safer from oblivion, though he number
  Full seventy cerements for a coverlid.
These Dead be seeds of life, and shall encumber
  The sad heart of the land until it loose
The clammy clods and let out the Spring-growth
  In beatific green through every bruise.
The tyrant should take heed to what he doth,
  Since every victim-carrion turns to use,
And drives a chariot, like a god made wroth,
  Against each piled injustice. Ay, the least,
Dead for Italia, not in vain has died;
  Though many vainly, ere life's struggle ceased,
To mad dissimilar ends have swerved aside;
  Each grave her nationality has pieced
By its own majestic breadth, and fortified
  And pinned it deeper to the soil. Forlorn
Of thanks be, therefore, no one of these graves!
  Not Hers,—who, at her husband's side, in scorn,
Outfaced the whistling shot and hissing waves,
  Until she felt her little babe unborn
Recoil, within her, from the violent staves
  And bloodhounds of the world,—at which, her life
Dropt inwards from her eyes and followed it
  Beyond the hunters. Garibaldi's wife

And child died so.   And now, the seaweeds fit
   Her body, like a proper shroud and coif,
And murmurously the ebbing waters grit
   The little pebbles while she lies interred
In the sea-sand.   Perhaps, ere dying thus,
   She looked up in his face (which never stirred
From its clenched anguish) as to make excuse
   For leaving him for his, if so she erred.
He well remembers that she could not choose.

   A memorable grave! Another is
At Genoa.   There, a king may fitly lie,
   Who, bursting that heroic heart of his
At lost Novara, that he could not die
   (Though thrice into the cannon's eyes for this
He plunged his shuddering steed, and felt the sky
   Reel back between the fire-shocks), stripped away
The ancestral ermine ere the smoke had cleared,
   And, naked to the soul, that none might say
His kingship covered what was base and bleared
   With treason, went out straight an exile, yea,
An exiled patriot.   Let him be revered.

   Yea, verily, Charles Albert has died well;
And if he lived not all so, as one spoke,
   The sin pass softly with the passing-bell:
For he was shriven, I think, in cannon-smoke,

And, taking off his crown, made visible
A hero's forehead.  Shaking Austria's yoke
   He shattered his own hand and heart.  "So best,"
His last words were upon his lonely bed,
   I do not end like popes and dukes at least—
"Thank God for it."  And now that he is dead,
   Admitting it is proved and manifest
That he was worthy, with a discrowned head,
   To measure heights with patriots, let them stand
Beside the man in his Oporto shroud,
   And each vouchsafe to take him by the hand,
And kiss him on the cheek, and say aloud,—
   "Thou, too, hast suffered for our native land!
My brother, thou art one of us! be proud."

   Still, graves, when Italy is talked upon.
Still, still, the patriot's tomb, the stranger's hate.
   Still Niobe! still fainting in the sun,
By whose most dazzling arrows violate
   Her beauteous offspring perished! has she won
Nothing but garlands for the graves, from Fate?
   Nothing but death-songs?—Yes, be it understood
Life throbs in noble Piedmont! while the feet
   Of Rome's clay image, dabbled soft in blood,
Grow flat with dissolution and, as meet,
   Will soon be shovelled off like other mud,

To leave the passage free in church and street.
    And I, who first took hope up in this song,
Because a child was singing one . . . behold,
    The hope and omen were not, haply, wrong!
Poets are soothsayers still, like those of old
    Who studied flights of doves; and creatures young
And tender, mighty meanings may unfold.

    The sun strikes, through the windows, up the floor;
Stand out in it, my own young Florentine,
    Not two years old, and let me see thee more!
It grows along thy amber curls, to shine
    Brighter than elsewhere. Now, look straight before,
And fix thy brave blue English eyes on mine,
    And from my soul, which fronts the future so,
With unabashed and unabated gaze,
    Teach me to hope for, what the angels know
When they smile clear as thou dost. Down God's ways
    With just alighted feet, between the snow
And snowdrops, where a little lamb may graze,
    Thou hast no fear, my lamb, about the road,
Albeit in our vain-glory we assume
    That, less than we have, thou hast learnt of God.
Stand out, my blue-eyed prophet!—thou, to whom
    The earliest world-day light that ever flowed,
Through Casa Guidi Windows chanced to come!

Now shake the glittering nimbus of thy hair,
And be God's witness that the elemental
  New springs of life are gushing everywhere
To cleanse the watercourses, and prevent all
  Concrete obstructions which infest the air!
That earth's alive, and gentle or ungentle
  Motions within her, signify but growth!—
The ground swells greenest o'er the labouring moles.

Howe'er the uneasy world is vexed and wroth,
Young children, lifted high on parent souls,
  Look round them with a smile upon the mouth,
And take for music every bell that tolls;
  (WHO said we should be better if like these?)
But *we* sit murmuring for the future though
  Posterity is smiling on our knees,
Convicting us of folly. Let us go—
  We will trust God. The blank interstices
Men take for ruins, He will build into
  With pillared marbles rare, or knit across
With generous arches, till the fane's complete.
  This world has no perdition, if some loss.

Such cheer I gather from thy smiling, Sweet!
  The self-same cherub-faces which emboss
The Vail, lean inward to the Mercy-seat.

# POEMS
# BEFORE CONGRESS

# PREFACE.

THESE poems were written under the pressure of the events they indicate, after a residence in Italy of so many years that the present triumph of great principles is heightened to the writer's feelings by the disastrous issue of the last movement, witnessed from "Casa Guidi Windows" in 1849. Yet, if the verses should appear to English readers too pungently rendered to admit of a patriotic respect to the English sense of things, I will not excuse myself on such grounds, nor on the ground of my attachment to the Italian people and my admiration of their heroic constancy and union. What I have written has simply been written because I love truth and justice *quand même*,—" more than Plato" and Plato's country, more than Dante and Dante's country, more even than Shakespeare and Shakespeare's country.

And if patriotism means the flattery of one's nation in every case, then the patriot, take it as you please, is merely the courtier which I am not, though I have written "Napoleon III. in Italy." It is time to limit the significance of certain terms, or to enlarge the significance of certain things. Nationality is excellent in its place ; and the instinct of self-love is the root of a man, which will develop into sacrificial virtues. But all the virtues are means and uses ; and, if we hinder their tendency to growth and expansion, we both destroy them as virtues, and degrade them to that rankest species of corruption reserved for the most noble organizations. For instance,—non-intervention in the affairs of neighbouring states is a high political virtue ; but non-intervention does not mean, passing by on the other side when your neighbour falls among thieves,—or Phariseeism would recover it from Christianity. Freedom itself is virtue, as well as privilege ; but freedom of the seas does not mean piracy, nor freedom of the land, brigandage ; nor freedom of the senate, freedom to cudgel a dissident member ; nor freedom of the press, freedom to calumniate and lie. So, if patriotism be a virtue indeed, it cannot mean an exclusive devotion to our country's interests,—for that is only another form of devotion to personal interests, family interests, or provincial interests, all of which, if not driven past themselves, are vulgar and immoral objects. Let us put away the Little Peddlingtonism unworthy of a great nation, and too prevalent among us. If the man who does not look beyond this natural life is of a somewhat narrow order, what must be the man who does not look beyond his own frontier or his own sea?

I confess that I dream of the day when an English statesman shall arise with a heart too large for England ; having courage in the face of his countrymen to assert of some suggested policy,—" This is good for your trade ; this is necessary for your domination : but it will vex a people hard by ; it will hurt a people farther off; it will profit nothing to the general humanity : therefore, away with it !—it is not for you or for me." When a British minister dares speak so, and when a British public applauds him speaking, then shall the nation be glorious, and her praise, instead of exploding from within, from loud civic mouths, come to her from without, as all worthy praise must, from the alliances she has fostered and the populations she has saved.

And poets who write of the events of that time shall not need to justify themselves in prefaces for ever so little jarring of the national sentiment imputable to their rhymes.

ROME : *February* 1860.

# NAPOLEON III. IN ITALY.

### I.

EMPEROR, Emperor!
From the centre to the shore,
 From the Seine back to the Rhine,
Stood eight millions up and swore
 By their manhood's right divine
So to elect and legislate,
 This man should renew the line
Broken in a strain of fate
And leagued kings at Waterloo,
When the people's hands let go.
 Emperor
 Evermore.

### II.

With a universal shout
They took the old regalia out
From an open grave that day;
 From a grave that would not close,

Where the first Napoleon lay
   Expectant, in repose,
As still as Merlin, with his conquering face
   Turned up in its unquenchable appeal
To men and heroes of the advancing race,—
   Prepared to set the seal
Of what has been on what shall be.
       Emperor
       Evermore.

### III.

The thinkers stood aside
   To let the nation act.
   Some hated the new-constituted fact
Of empire, as pride treading on their pride.
Some quailed, lest what was poisonous in the past
   Should graft itself in that Druidic bough
     On this green Now.
Some cursed, because at last
The open heavens to which they had looked in vain
For many a golden fall of marvellous rain
Were closed in brass; and some
Wept on because a gone thing could not come;
And some were silent, doubting all things for
That popular conviction,—evermore
       Emperor.

IV.

That day I did not hate
   Nor doubt, nor quail nor curse.
I, reverencing the people, did not bate
My reverence of their deed and oracle,
Nor vainly prate
   Of better and of worse
Against the great conclusion of their will.
   And yet, O voice and verse,
Which God set in me to acclaim and sing
Conviction, exaltation, aspiration,
We gave no music to the patent thing,
   Nor spared a holy rhythm to throb and swim
   About the name of him
Translated to the sphere of domination
   By democratic passion!
I was not used, at least,
   Nor can be, now or then,
To stroke the ermine beast
   On any kind of throne
   (Though builded by a nation for its own),
And swell the surging choir for kings of men—
     "Emperor
       Evermore."

## V.

But now, Napoleon, now
That, leaving far behind the purple throng
  Of vulgar monarchs, thou
  Tread'st higher in thy deed
  Than stair of throne can lead,
  To help in the hour of wrong
  The broken hearts of nations to be strong,—
  Now, lifted as thou art
  To the level of pure song,
We stand to meet thee on these Alpine snows!
  And while the palpitating peaks break out
Ecstatic from somnambular repose
  With answers to the presence and the shout,
We, poets of the people, who take part
  With elemental justice, natural right,
Join in our echoes also, nor refrain.
  We meet thee, O Napoleon, at this height
At last, and find thee great enough to praise.
Receive the poet's chrism, which smells beyond
  The priest's, and pass thy ways;—
An English poet warns thee to maintain
God's word, not England's:—let His truth be true
And all men liars! with His truth respond
To all men's lie. Exalt the sword and smite

On that long anvil of the Apennine
Where Austria forged the Italian chain in view
Of seven consenting nations, sparks of fine
    Admonitory light,
Till men's eyes wink before convictions new.
Flash in God's justice to the world's amaze,
Sublime Deliverer!—after many days
Found worthy of the deed thou art come to do—
    Emperor.
    Evermore.

## VI.

But Italy, my Italy,
  Can it last, this gleam?
Can she live and be strong,
  Or is it another dream
Like the rest we have dreamed so long?
  And shall it, must it be,
That after the battle-cloud has broken
  She will die off again
  Like the rain,
Or like a poet's song
  Sung of her, sad at the end
Because her name is Italy,—
  Die and count no friend?
Is it true,—may it be spoken,—

That she who has lain so still,
With a wound in her breast,
And a flower in her hand,
And a grave-stone under her head,
   While every nation at will
Beside her has dared to stand,
And flout her with pity and scorn,
   Saying "She is at rest,
She is fair, she is dead,
And, leaving room in her stead
To Us who are later born,
   This is certainly best!"
Saying "Alas, she is fair,
Very fair, but dead,—give place,
And so we have room for the race."
—Can it be true, be true,
That she lives anew?
That she rises up at the shout of her sons,
   At the trumpet of France,
And lives anew?—is it true
   That she has not moved in a trance,
As in Forty-eight?
   When her eyes were troubled with blood
Till she knew not friend from foe,
Till her hand was caught in a strait
Of her cerement and baffled so

From doing the deed she would;
And her weak foot stumbled across
The grave of a king,
And down she dropt at heavy loss,
   And we gloomily covered her face and said,
"We have dreamed the thing;
   She is not alive, but dead."


### VII.

Now, shall we say
   Our Italy lives indeed?
And if it were not for the beat and bray
Of drum and trump of martial men,
Should we feel the underground heave and strain,
   Where heroes left their dust as a seed
Sure to emerge one day?
And if it were not for the rhythmic march
   Of France and Piedmont's double hosts,
   Should we hear the ghosts
Thrill through ruined aisle and arch,
   Throb along the frescoed wall,
Whisper an oath by that divine
They left in picture, book, and stone,
   That Italy is not dead at all?
Ay, if it were not for the tears in our eyes,

These tears of a sudden passionate joy,
    Should we see her arise
From the place where the wicked are overthrown,
Italy, Italy—loosed at length
    From the tyrant's thrall,
Pale and calm in her strength?
Pale as the silver cross of Savoy
When the hand that bears the flag is brave,
And not a breath is stirring, save
    What is blown
Over the war-trump's lip of brass,
Ere Garibaldi forces the pass!


### VIII.

    Ay, it is so, even so.
    Ay, and it shall be so.
Each broken stone that long ago
She flung behind her as she went
In discouragement and bewilderment
Through the cairns of Time, and missed her way
Between to-day and yesterday,
    Up springs a living man.
And each man stands with his face in the light
    Of his own drawn sword,
    Ready to do what a hero can.

Wall to sap, or river to ford,
Cannon to front, or foe to pursue,
Still ready to do, and sworn to be true,
   As a man and a patriot can.
   Piedmontese, Neapolitan,
Lombard, Tuscan, Romagnole,
Each man's body having a soul,—
Count how many they stand,
All of them sons of the land,
   Every live man there
Allied to a dead man below,
   And the deadest with blood to spare
To quicken a living hand
In case it should ever be slow.
Count how many they come
To the beat of Piedmont's drum,
   With faces keener and grayer
   Than swords of the Austrian slayer,
All set against the foe.
    "Emperor
    Evermore."

## IX.

Out of the dust where they ground them;
  Out of the holes where they dogged them;
Out of the hulks where they wound them

In iron, tortured and flogged them;
Out of the streets where they chased them,
 Taxed them, and then bayonetted them;
Out of the homes where they spied on them
 (Using their daughters and wives);
 Out of the church where they fretted them,
Rotted their souls and debased them,
 Trained them to answer with knives,
Then cursed them all at their prayers!—
Out of cold lands, not theirs,
Where they exiled them, starved them, lied on them
Back they come like a wind, in vain
 Cramped up in the hills, that roars its road
The stronger into the open plain,
Or like a fire that burns the hotter
 And longer for the crust of cinder,
Serving better the ends of the potter;
 Or like a restrainèd word of God,
 Fulfilling itself by what seems to hinder.
   "Emperor
   Evermore."

### X.

 Shout for France and Savoy!
  Shout for the helper and doer.
 Shout for the good sword's ring,

Shout for the thought still truer.
Shout for the spirits at large
Who passed for the dead this spring,
   Whose living glory is sure.
Shout for France and Savoy!
Shout for the council and charge!
   Shout for the head of Cavour;
And shout for the heart of a King
That's great with a nation's joy!
   Shout for France and Savoy!


### XI.

Take up the child, Macmahon, though
   Thy hand be red
   From Magenta's dead,
And riding on, in front of the troop,
   In the dust of the whirlwind of war
Through the gate of the city of Milan, stoop
And take up the child to thy saddle-bow,
Nor fear the touch as soft as a flower of his smile
   as clear as a star!
Thou hast a right to the child, we say,
Since the women are weeping for joy as they
Who, by thy help and from this day,
   Shall be happy mothers indeed.

They are raining flowers from terrace and roof:
　　Take up the flower in the child.
While the shout goes up of a nation freed
　　And heroically self-reconciled,
Till the snow on that peaked Alp aloof
Starts, as feeling God's finger anew,
And all those cold white marble fires
Of mounting saints on the Duomo-spires
　　Flicker against the Blue.
　　　　" Emperor
　　　　Evermore."


### XII.

　　Ay, it is He,
Who rides at the King's right hand!
Leave room to his horse and draw to the side,
　　Nor press too near in the ecstasy
Of a newly delivered impassioned land:
　　He is moved, you see,
He who has done it all.
They call it a cold stern face;
　　But this is Italy
Who rises up to her place!—
For this he fought in his youth,
Of this he dreamed in the past;

The lines of the resolute mouth
Tremble a little at last.
Cry, he has done it all!
"Emperor
Evermore."

### XIII.

It is not strange that he did it.
    Though the deed may seem to strain
To the wonderful, unpermitted,
    For such as lead and reign.
But he is strange, this man:
    The people's instinct found him
(A wind in the dark that ran
Through a chink where was no door),
    And elected him and crowned him
Emperor
Evermore.

### XIV.

Autocrat? let them scoff,
    Who fail to comprehend
That a ruler incarnate of
    The people must transcend

All common king-born kings ;
These subterranean springs
A sudden outlet winning
   Have special virtues to spend.
The people's blood runs through him,
   Dilates from head to foot,
   Creates him absolute,
And from this great beginning
   Evokes a greater end
To justify and renew him—
      Emperor
      Evermore.


XV.

What! did any maintain
That God or the people (think !)
Could make a marvel in vain ?—
   Out of the water-jar there,
Draw wine that none could drink ?
Is this a man like the rest,
   This miracle, made unaware
   By a rapture of popular air,
And caught to the place that was best ?
You think he could barter and cheat
   As vulgar diplomates use,

With the people's heart in his breast?
Prate a lie into shape
Lest truth should cumber the road;
   Play at the fast and loose
Till the world is strangled with tape;
Maim the soul's complete
   To fit the hole of a toad;
And filch the dogman's meat
   To feed the offspring of God?

### XVI.

Nay, but he, this wonder,
   He cannot palter nor prate,
Though many around him and under,
With intellects trained to the curve,
Distrust him in spirit and nerve
   Because his meaning is straight.
Measure him ere he depart
   With those who have governed and led;
Larger so much by the heart,
   Larger so much by the head.
      Emperor
      Evermore.

## XVII.

He holds that, consenting or dissident,
   Nations must move with the time;
Assumes that crime with a precedent
   Doubles the guilt of the crime;
—Denies that a slaver's bond,
   Or a treaty signed by knaves
(*Quorum magna pars*, and beyond
Was one of an honest name),
Gives an inexpugnable claim
   To abolish men into slaves.
      Emperor
      Evermore.

## XVIII.

He will not swagger nor boast
   Of his country's meeds, in a tone
Missuiting a great man most
   If such should speak of his own;
Nor will he act, on her side,
   From motives baser, indeed,
Than a man of a noble pride
   Can avow for himself at need;

Never, for lucre or laurels,
   Or custom, though such should be rife,
Adapting the smaller morals
   To measure the larger life.
He, though the merchants persuade,
   And the soldiers are eager for strife,
Finds not his country in quarrels
   Only to find her in trade,—
While still he accords her such honour
   As never to flinch for her sake
Where men put service upon her,
   Found heavy to undertake
And scarcely like to be paid:
Believing a nation may act
   Unselfishly—shiver a lance
(As the least of her sons may, in fact)
   And not for a cause of finance.
       Emperor
       Evermore.

### XIX.

  Great is he
Who uses his greatness for all.
His name shall stand perpetually
   As a name to applaud and cherish,

Not only within the civic wall
For the loyal, but also without
   For the generous and free.
   Just is he,
Who is just for the popular due
   As well as the private debt.
The praise of nations ready to perish
Fall on him,—crown him in view
   Of tyrants caught in the net,
And statesmen dizzy with fear and doubt!
And though, because they are many,
   And he is merely one,
And nations selfish and cruel
Heap up the inquisitor's fuel
   To kill the body of high intents,
And burn great deeds from their place,
Till this, the greatest of any,
   May seem imperfectly done;
   Courage, whoever circumvents!
Courage, courage, whoever is base!
The soul of a high intent, be it known,
Can die no more than any soul
Which God keeps by Him under the throne;
And this, at whatever interim,
   Shall live, and be consummated
Into the being of deeds made whole.

Courage, courage! happy is he,
  Of whom (himself among the dead
  And silent) this word shall be said:
—That he might have had the world with him,
  But chose to side with suffering men,
  And had the world against him when
He came to deliver Italy.
        Emperor
        Evermore.

## THE DANCE.

### I.

You remember down at Florence our Cascine,
 Where the people on the feast-days walk and drive,
And, through the trees, long-drawn in many a green
  way,
 O'er-roofing hum and murmur like a hive,
 The river and the mountains look alive?

### II.

You remember the piazzone there, the stand-place
 Of carriages a-brim with Florence Beauties,
Who lean and melt to music as the band plays,
 Or smile and chat with someone who a-foot is,
 Or on horseback, in observance of male duties?

### III.

'T is so pretty, in the afternoons of summer,
  So many gracious faces brought together!
Call it rout, or call it concert, they have come here,
  In the floating of the fan and of the feather,
  To reciprocate with beauty the fine weather.

### IV.

While the flower-girls offer nosegays (because *they* too
  Go with other sweets) at every carriage-door;
Here, by shake of a white finger, signed away to
  Some next buyer, who sits buying score on score,
  Piling roses upon roses evermore.

### V.

And last season, when the French camp had its station
  In the meadow-ground, things quickened and grew
      gayer
Through the mingling of the liberating nation
  With this people; groups of Frenchmen everywhere,
  Strolling, gazing, judging lightly—"who was fair."

VI.

Then the noblest lady present took upon her
   To speak nobly from her carriage for the rest :
" Pray these officers from France to do us honour
   By dancing with us straightway."   The request
   Was gravely apprehended as addressed.

VII.

And the men of France, bareheaded, bowing lowly,
   Led out each a proud signora to the space
Which the startled crowd had rounded for them—
      slowly,
   Just a touch of still emotion in his face,
   Not presuming, through the symbol, on the grace.

VIII.

There was silence in the people : some lips trembled,
   But none jested.   Broke the music, at a glance :
And the daughters of our princes, thus assembled,
   Stepped the measure with the gallant sons of France,
   Hush ! it might have been a Mass, and not a dance.

## IX.

And they danced there till the blue that overskied us
   Swooned with passion, though the footing seemed
      sedate;
And the mountains, heaving mighty hearts beside us,
   Sighed a rapture in a shadow, to dilate,
   And touch the holy stone where Dante sate.

## X.

Then the sons of France, bareheaded, lowly bowing,
   Led the ladies back where kinsmen of the south
Stood, received them; till, with burst of overflowing
   Feeling—husbands, brothers, Florence's male youth,
   Turned, and kissed the martial strangers mouth to
      mouth.

## XI.

And a cry went up, a cry from all that people!
   —You have heard a people cheering, you suppose,
For the Member, mayor . . . with chorus from the
      steeple?
   This was different: scarce as loud, perhaps (who
      knows?),
   For we saw wet eyes around us ere the close.

XII.

And we felt as if a nation, too long borne in
   By hard wrongers,—comprehending in such attitude
That God had spoken somewhere since the morning,
   That men were somehow brothers, by no platitude,—
   Cried exultant in great wonder and free gratitude.

## *A TALE OF VILLAFRANCA.*

#### TOLD IN TUSCANY.

### I.

My little son, my Florentine,
   Sit down beside my knee,
And I will tell you why the sign
   Of joy which flushed our Italy
Has faded since but yesternight;
And why your Florence of delight
   Is mourning as you see.

### II.

A great man (who was crowned one day)
   Imagined a great Deed:
He shaped it out of cloud and clay,
   He touched it finely till the seed
Possessed the flower: from heart and brain
He fed it with large thoughts humane,
   To help a people's need.

### III.

He brought it out into the sun —
   They blessed it to his face:
"O great pure Deed, that hast undone
   So many bad and base!
O generous Deed, heroic Deed,
Come forth, be perfected, succeed,
   Deliver by God's grace."

### IV.

Then sovereigns, statesmen, north and south,
   Rose up in wrath and fear,
And cried, protesting by one mouth,
   "What monster have we here?
A great Deed at this hour of day?
A great just Deed—and not for pay?
   Absurd,—or insincere."

### V.

"And if sincere, the heavier blow
   In that case we shall bear,
For where 's our blessed 'status quo,'
   Our holy treaties, where,—
Our rights to sell a race, or buy,
Protect and pillage, occupy,
   And civilize despair?"

VI.

Some muttered that the great Deed meant
　　A great pretext to sin;
And others, the pretext, so lent,
　　Was heinous (to begin).
Volcanic terms of "great" and "just"?
Admit such tongues of flame, the crust
　　Of time and law falls in.

VII.

A great Deed in this world of ours?
　　Unheard of the pretence is:
It threatens plainly the great Powers;
　　Is fatal in all senses.
A just Deed in the world?—call out
The rifles! be not slack about
　　The national defences.

VIII.

And many murmured, "From this source
　　What red blood must be poured!"
And some rejoined, "'T is even worse;
　　What red tape is ignored!"
All cursed the Doer for an evil
Called here, enlarging on the Devil,—
　　There, monkeying the Lord!

### IX.

Some said it could not be explained,
    Some, could not be excused;
And others, " Leave it unrestrained,
    Gehenna's self is loosed."
And all cried "Crush it, maim it, gag it!
Set dog-toothed lies to tear it ragged,
    Truncated and traduced!"

### X.

But HE stood sad before the sun
    (The peoples felt their fate).
"The world is many,—I am one;
    My great Deed was too great.
God's fruit of justice ripens slow:
Men's souls are narrow; let them grow.
    My brothers, we must wait."

### XI.

The tale is ended, child of mine,
    Turned graver at my knee.
They say your eyes, my Florentine,
    Are English: it may be.
And yet I 've marked as blue a pair
Following the doves across the square
    At Venice by the sea.

### XII.

Ah child! ah child! I cannot say
   A word more.　You conceive
The reason now, why just to-day
   We see our Florence grieve.
Ah child, look up into the sky!
In this low world, where great Deeds die,
   What matter if we live?

## *A COURT LADY.*

### I.

HER hair was tawny with gold, her eyes with purple were dark,
Her cheeks' pale opal burnt with a red and restless spark.

### II.

Never was lady of Milan nobler in name and in race;
Never was lady of Italy fairer to see in the face.

### III.

Never was lady on earth more true as woman and wife,
Larger in judgment and instinct, prouder in manners and life.

### IV.

She stood in the early morning, and said to her
    maidens "Bring
That silken robe made ready to wear at the Court of
    the King.

### V.

"Bring me the clasps of diamond, lucid, clear of the
    mote,
Clasp me the large at the waist, and clasp me the small
    at the throat.

### VI.

"Diamonds to fasten the hair, and diamonds to fasten
    the sleeves,
Laces to drop from their rays, like a powder of snow
    from the eaves."

### VII.

Gorgeous she entered the sunlight which gathered her
    up in a flame,
While, straight in her open carriage, she to the hospital
    came.

### VIII.

In she went at the door, and gazing from end to
    end,
"Many and low are the pallets, but each is the place
    of a friend."

### IX.

Up she passed through the wards, and stood at a
    young man's bed:
Bloody the band on his brow, and livid the droop of
    his head.

### X.

"Art thou a Lombard, my brother? Happy art thou,"
    she cried,
And smiled like Italy on him: he dreamed in her face
    and died.

### XI.

Pale with his passing soul, she went on still to a
    second:
He was a grave hard man, whose years by dungeons
    were reckoned.

XII.

Wounds in his body were sore, wounds in his life were sorer.
"Art thou a Romagnole?" Her eyes drove lightnings before her.

XIII.

"Austrian and priest had joined to double and tighten the cord
Able to bind thee, O strong one,—free by the stroke of a sword.

XIV.

"Now be grave for the rest of us, using the life overcast
To ripen our wine of the present (too new) in glooms of the past."

XV.

Down she stepped to a pallet where lay a face like a girl's,
Young, and pathetic with dying,—a deep black hole in the curls.

### XVI.

"Art thou from Tuscany, brother? and seest thou, dreaming in pain,
Thy mother stand in the piazza, searching the List of the slain?"

### XVII.

Kind as a mother herself, she touched his cheeks with her hands:
"Blessed is she who has borne thee, although she should weep as she stands."

### XVIII.

On she passed to a Frenchman, his arm carried off by a ball:
Kneeling,—"O more than my brother! how shall I thank thee for all?

### XIX.

"Each of the heroes around us has fought for his land and line,
But thou hast fought for a stranger, in hate of a wrong not thine.

XX.

"Happy are all free peoples, too strong to be dispossessed.
But blessed are those among nations who dare to be strong for the rest!"


XXI.

Ever she passed on her way, and came to a couch where pined
One with a face from Venetia, white with a hope out of mind.


XXII.

Long she stood and gazed, and twice she tried at the name,
But two great crystal tears were all that faltered and came.


XXIII.

Only a tear for Venice?—she turned as in passion and loss,
And stooped to his forehead and kissed it, as if she were kissing the cross.

### XXIV.

Faint with that strain of heart she moved on then to another,
Stern and strong in his death. "And dost thou suffer, my brother?"

### XXV.

Holding his hands in hers:—"Out of the Piedmont lion
Cometh the sweetness of freedom! sweetest to live or to die on."

### XXVI.

Holding his cold rough hands,—"Well, oh well have ye done
In noble, noble Piedmont, who would not be noble alone."

### XXVII.

Back he fell while she spoke. She rose to her feet with a spring,—
"That was a Piedmontese! and this is the Court of the King."

## AN AUGUST VOICE.

"Una voce augusta."—*Monitore Toscano.*

### I.

You 'll take back your Grand-duke?
   I made the treaty upon it.
Just venture a quiet rebuke;
   Dall' Ongaro write him a sonnet;
Ricasoli gently explain
   Some need of the constitution:
He 'll swear to it over again,
   Providing an "easy solution."
You 'll call back the Grand-duke. .

### II.

You 'll take back your Grand-duke?
   I promised the Emperor Francis
To argue the case by his book,
   And ask you to meet his advances.

The Ducal cause, we know
   (Whether you or he be the wronger),
Has very strong points;—although
   Your bayonets, there, have stronger.
You 'll call back the Grand-duke.


You 'll take back your Grand-duke?
   He is not pure altogether.
For instance, the oath which he took
   (In the Forty-eight rough weather)
He 'd "nail your flag to his mast,"
   Then softly scuttled the boat you
Hoped to escape in at last,
   And both by a "Proprio motu."
You 'll call back the Grand-duke.

### IV.

You 'll take back your Grand-duke?
   The scheme meets nothing to shock it
In this smart letter, look,
   We found in Radetsky's pocket;
Where his Highness in sprightly style
   Of the flower of his Tuscans wrote,

"These heads be the hottest in file;
   Pray shoot them the quickest." Quote,
And call back the Grand-duke.

### v.

You'll take back your Grand-duke?
   There *are* some things to object to.
He cheated, betrayed, and forsook,
   Then called in the foe to protect you.
He taxed you for wines and for meats
   Throughout that eight years' pastime
Of Austria's drum in your streets—
   Of course you remember the last time
You called back your Grand-duke?

### vi.

You'll take back the Grand-duke?
   It is not race he is poor in,
Although he never could brook
   The patriot cousin at Turin.
His love of kin you discern,
   By his hate of your flag and me—
So decidedly apt to turn
   All colours at the sight of the Three.*
You'll call back the Grand-duke.

* The Italian tricolor: red, green, and white.

### VII.

You 'll take back your Grand-duke?
   'T was weak that he fled from the Pitti;
But consider how little he shook
   At thought of bombarding your city!
And, balancing that with this,
   The Christian rule is plain for us;
. . Or the Holy Father's Swiss
   Have shot his Perugians in vain for us.
You 'll call back the Grand-duke.

### VIII.

Pray take back your Grand-duke.
   —I, too, have suffered persuasion.
All Europe, raven and rook,
   Screeched at me armed for your nation.
Your cause in my heart struck spurs;
   I swept such warnings aside for you:
My very child's eyes, and Hers,
   Grew like my brother's who died for you.
You 'll call back the Grand-duke?

### IX.

You 'll take back your Grand-duke?
   My French fought nobly with reason,—

Left many a Lombardy nook
   Red as with wine out of season.
Little we grudged what was done there,
   Paid freely your ransom of blood:
Our heroes stark in the sun there
   We would not recall if we could.
You'll call back the Grand-duke?


X.

You'll take back your Grand-duke?
   His son rode fast as he got off
That day on the enemy's hook,
   When *I* had an epaulette shot off.
Though splashed (as I saw him afar—no
   Near) by those ghastly rains,
The mark, when you've washed him in Arno,
   Will scarcely be larger than Cain's.
You'll call back the Grand-duke?


XI.

You'll take back your Grand-duke?
   'T will be so simple, quite beautiful:
The shepherd recovers his crook,
      . . . If you should be sheep, and dutiful.

I spoke a word worth chalking
   On Milan's wall—but stay,
Here's Poniatowsky talking,—
   You'll listen to *him* to-day,
And call back the Grand-duke.

### XII.

You'll take back your Grand-duke?
   Observe, there's no one to force it,—
Unless the Madonna, Saint Luke
   Drew for you, choose to endorse it.
*I* charge you, by great Saint Martino
   And prodigies quickened by wrong,
Remember your Dead on Ticino;
   Be worthy, be constant, be strong—
Bah!—call back the Grand-duke!!

## *CHRISTMAS GIFTS.*

ὡς βασιλεῖ, ὡς θεῷ, ὡς νεκρῷ.
GREGORY NAZIANZEN.

I.

THE Pope on Christmas Day
  Sits in Saint Peter's chair;
But the peoples murmur and say
  "Our souls are sick and forlorn,
And who will show us where
  Is the stable where Christ was born?"

II.

The star is lost in the dark;
  The manger is lost in the straw;
The Christ cries faintly . . . hark! . . .
  Through bands that swaddle and strangle—
But the Pope in the chair of awe
  Looks down the great quadrangle.

III.

The Magi kneel at his foot,
   Kings of the East and West,
But, instead of the angels (mute
   Is the "Peace on earth" of their song),
The peoples, perplexed and opprest,
   Are sighing "How long, how long?"

IV.

And, instead of the kine, bewilder in
   Shadow of aisle and dome,
The bear who tore up the children,
   The fox who burnt up the corn,
And the wolf who suckled at Rome
   Brothers to slay and to scorn.

V.

Cardinals left and right of him,
   Worshippers round and beneath,
The silver trumpets at sight of him
   Thrill with a musical blast:
But the people say through their teeth,
   "Trumpets? we wait for the Last!"

## VI.

He sits in the place of the Lord,
    And asks for the gifts of the time;
Gold, for the haft of a sword
    To win back Romagna averse,
Incense, to sweeten a crime,
    And myrrh, to embitter a curse.

## VII.

Then a king of the West said "Good!—
    I bring thee the gifts of the time;
Red, for the patriot's blood,
    Green, for the martyr's crown,
White, for the dew and the rime,
    When the morning of God comes down."

## VIII.

—O mystic tricolor bright!
    The Pope's heart quailed like a man's;
The cardinals froze at the sight,
    Bowing their tonsures hoary:
And the eyes in the peacock-fans
    Winked at the alien glory.

IX.

But the peoples exclaimed in hope,
   "Now blessed be he who has brought
These gifts of the time to the Pope,
   When our souls were sick and forlorn.
—And *here* is the star we sought,
   To show us where Christ was born!"

## ITALY AND THE WORLD.

### I.

FLORENCE, Bologna, Parma, Modena:
   When you named them a year ago,
So many graves reserved by God, in a
   Day of Judgment, you seemed to know,
To open and let out the resurrection.

### II.

And meantime (you made your reflection
   If you were English), was nought to be done
But sorting sables, in predilection
   For all those martyrs dead and gone,
Till the new earth and heaven made ready.

III.

And if your politics were not heady,
    Violent, . . . " Good," you added, " good
In all things !   Mourn on sure and steady.
    Churchyard thistles are wholesome food
For our European wandering asses.



IV.

"The date of the resurrection passes
    Human foreknowledge : men unborn
Will gain by it (even in the lower classes),
    But none of these.   It is not the morn
Because the cock of France is crowing.



V.

"Cocks crow at midnight, seldom knowing
    Starlight from dawn-light !  't is a mad
Poor creature."   Here you paused, and growing
    Scornful,—suddenly, let us add,
The trumpet sounded, the graves were open.

## VI.

Life and life and life! agrope in
   The dusk of death, warm hands, stretched out
For swords, proved more life still to hope in,
   Beyond and behind. Arise with a shout,
Nation of Italy, slain and buried!

## VII.

Hill to hill and turret to turret
   Flashing the tricolor,—newly created
Beautiful Italy, calm, unhurried,
   Rise heroic and renovated,
Rise to the final restitution.

## VIII.

Rise; prefigure the grand solution
   Of earth's municipal, insular schisms,—
Statesmen draping self-love's conclusion
   In cheap vernacular patriotisms,
Unable to give up Judæa for Jesus.

### IX.

Bring us the higher example; release us
   Into the larger coming time:
And into Christ's broad garment piece us
   Rags of virtue as poor as crime,
National selfishness, civic vaunting.

### X.

No more Jew nor Greek then,—taunting
   Nor taunted;—no more England nor France!
But one confederate brotherhood planting
   One flag only, to mark the advance,
Onward and upward, of all humanity.

### XI.

For civilization perfected
   Is fully developed Christianity.
"Measure the frontier," shall it be said,
   "Count the ships," in national vanity?
—Count the nation's heart-beats sooner.

### XII.

For, though behind by a cannon or schooner,
    That nation still is predominant
Whose pulse beats quickest in zeal to oppugn or
    Succour another, in wrong or want,
Passing the frontier in love and abhorrence.

### XIII.

Modena, Parma, Bologna, Florence,
    Open us out the wider way!
Dwarf in that chapel of old Saint Lawrence
    Your Michel Angelo's giant Day,
With the grandeur of this Day breaking o'er us!

### XIV.

Ye who, restrained as an ancient chorus,
    Mute while the coryphæus spake,
Hush your separate voices before us,
    Sink your separate lives for the sake
Of one sole Italy's living for ever!

## XV.

Givers of coat and cloak too,—never
    Grudging that purple of yours at the best,-
By your heroic will and endeavour
    Each sublimely dispossessed,
That all may inherit what each surrenders!

## XVI.

Earth shall bless you, O noble emenders
    On egotist nations! Ye shall lead
The plough of the world, and sow new splendours
    Into the furrow of things for seed,—
Ever the richer for what ye have given.

## XVII.

Lead us and teach us, till earth and heaven
    Grow larger around us and higher above.
Our sacrament-bread has a bitter leaven;
    We bait our traps with the name of love,
Till hate itself has a kinder meaning.

XVIII.

Oh, this world: this cheating and screening
   Of cheats! this conscience for candle-wicks,
Not beacon-fires! this overweening
   Of underhand diplomatical tricks,
Dared for the country while scorned for the counter!


XIX.

Oh, this envy of those who mount here,
   And oh, this malice to make them trip!
Rather quenching the fire there, drying the fount here,
   To frozen body and thirsty lip,
Than leave to a neighbour their ministration.


XX.

I cry aloud in my poet-passion,
   Viewing my England o'er Alp and sea.
I loved her more in her ancient fashion:
   She carries her rifles too thick for me
Who spares them so in the cause of a brother.

### XXI.

Suspicion, panic? end this pother.
    The sword, kept sheathless at peace-time, rusts.
None fears for himself while he feels for another:
    The brave man either fights or trusts,
And wears no mail in his private chamber.


### XXII.

Beautiful Italy! golden amber
    Warm with the kisses of lover and traitor!
Thou who hast drawn us on to remember,
    Draw us to hope now: let us be greater
By this new future than that old story.


### XXIII.

Till truer glory replaces all glory,
    As the torch grows blind at the dawn of day;
And the nations, rising up, their sorry
    And foolish sins shall put away,
As children their toys when the teacher enters.

XXIV.

Till Love's one centre devour these centres
  Of many self-loves; and the patriot's trick
To better his land by egotist ventures,
  Defamed from a virtue, shall make men sick,
As the scalp at the belt of some red hero.


XXV.

For certain virtues have dropped to zero,
  Left by the sun on the mountain's dewy side;
Churchman's charities, tender as Nero,
  Indian suttee, heathen suicide,
Service to rights divine, proved hollow:


XXVI.

And Heptarchy patriotisms must follow.
  —National voices, distinct yet dependent,
Ensphering each other, as swallow does swallow,
  With circles still widening and ever ascendant,
In multiform life to united progression,—

XXVII.

These shall remain. And when, in the session
   Of nations, the separate language is heard,
Each shall aspire, in sublime indiscretion,
   To help with a thought or exalt with a word
Less her own than her rival's honour.


XXVIII.

Each Christian nation shall take upon her
   The law of the Christian man in vast:
The crown of the getter shall fall to the donor,
   And last shall be first while first shall be last.
And to love best shall still be, to reign unsurpa

## *A CURSE FOR A NATION.*

### PROLOGUE.

I HEARD an angel speak last night,
    And he said "Write!
Write a Nation's curse for me,
And send it over the Western Sea."

I faltered, taking up the word:
    "Not so, my lord!
If curses must be, choose another
To send thy curse against my brother.

"For I am bound by gratitude,
    By love and blood,
To brothers of mine across the sea,
Who stretch out kindly hands to me."

"Therefore," the voice said, "shalt thou write
      My curse to-night.
From the summits of love a curse is driven,
As lightning is from the tops of heaven."


"Not so," I answered. "Evermore
      My heart is sore
For my own land's sins: for little feet
Of children bleeding along the street:


"For parked-up honours that gainsay
      The right of way:
For almsgiving through a door that is
Not open enough for two friends to kiss:


"For love of freedom which abates
      Beyond the Straits:
For patriot virtue starved to vice on
Self-praise, self-interest, and suspicion:


"For an oligarchic parliament,
      And bribes well-meant.
What curse to another land assign,
When heavy-souled for the sins of mine?"

"Therefore," the voice said, "shalt thou write
      My curse to-night.
Because thou hast strength to see and hate
A foul thing done *within* thy gate."


"Not so," I answered once again.
      "To curse, choose men.
For I, a woman, have only known
How the heart melts and the tears run down."


"Therefore," the voice said, "shalt thou write
      My curse to-night.
Some women weep and curse, I say
(And no one marvels), night and day.


"And thou shalt take their part to-night,
      Weep and write.
A curse from the depths of womanhood
Is very salt, and bitter, and good."


So thus I wrote, and mourned indeed,
      What all may read.
And thus, as was enjoined on me,
I send it over the Western Sea.

## THE CURSE.

### I.

Because ye have broken your own chain
      With the strain
Of brave men climbing a Nation's height,
Yet thence bear down with brand and thong
On souls of others,—for this wrong
      This is the curse. Write.

Because yourselves are standing straight
      In the state
Of Freedom's foremost acolyte,
Yet keep calm footing all the time
On writhing bond-slaves,—for this crime
      This is the curse. Write.

Because ye prosper in God's name,
      With a claim
To honour in the old world's sight,
Yet do the fiend's work perfectly
In strangling martyrs,—for this lie
      This is the curse. Write.

## II.

Ye shall watch while kings conspire
Round the people's smouldering fire,
   And, warm for your part,
Shall never dare—O shame!
To utter the thought into flame
   Which burns at your heart.
      This is the curse.  Write.

Ye shall watch while nations strive
With the bloodhounds, die or survive,
   Drop faint from their jaws,
Or throttle them backward to death;
And only under your breath
   Shall favour the cause.
      This is the curse.  Write.

Ye shall watch while strong men draw
The nets of feudal law
   To strangle the weak;
And, counting the sin for a sin,
Your soul shall be sadder within
   Than the word ye shall speak.
      This is the curse.  Write.

When good men are praying erect
That Christ may avenge his elect
   And deliver the earth,
The prayer in your ears, said low,
Shall sound like the tramp of a foe
   That's driving you forth.
      This is the curse. Write.


When wise men give you their praise,
They shall pause in the heat of the phrase,
   As if carried too far.
When ye boast your own charters kept true
Ye shall blush; for the thing which ye do
   Derides what ye are.
      This is the curse. Write.


When fools cast taunts at your gate,
Your scorn ye shall somewhat abate
   As ye look o'er the wall;
For your conscience, tradition, and name
Explode with a deadlier blame
   Than the worst of them all.
      This is the curse. Write.

## A CURSE FOR A NATION

Go, wherever ill deeds shall be done,
Go, plant your flag in the sun
   Beside the ill-doers!
And recoil from clenching the curse
Of God's witnessing Universe
   With a curse of yours.
      THIS is the curse. Write.

# LAST POEMS

# ADVERTISEMENT.

THESE Poems are given as they occur on a list drawn up last June. A few had already been printed in periodicals.

There is hardly such direct warrant for publishing the Translations; which were only intended, many years ago, to accompany and explain certain Engravings after ancient Gems, in the projected work of a friend, by whose kindness they are now recovered: but as two of the original series (the "Adonis" of Bion, and "Song to the Rose" from Achilles Tatius) have subsequently appeared, it is presumed that the remainder may not improperly follow.

A single recent version is added.

LONDON: *February* 1862.

TO "GRATEFUL FLORENCE,"

TO THE MUNICIPALITY HER REPRESENTATIVE,

AND TO TOMMASEO ITS SPOKESMAN,

MOST GRATEFULLY.

## LITTLE MATTIE.

### I.

DEAD! Thirteen a month ago!
    Short and narrow her life's walk;
Lover's love she could not know
    Even by a dream or talk:
Too young to be glad of youth,
    Missing honour, labour, rest,
And the warmth of a babe's mouth
    At the blossom of her breast.
Must you pity her for this
And for all the loss it is,
You, her mother, with wet face,
Having had all in your case?

### II.

Just so young but yesternight,
    Now she is as old as death.

Meek, obedient in your sight,
    Gentle to a beck or breath
Only on last Monday!   Yours,
    Answering you like silver bells
Lightly touched !   An hour matures :
    You can teach her nothing else.
She has seen the mystery hid
Under Egypt's pyramid :
By those eyelids pale and close
Now she knows what Rhamses knows.


### III.

Cross her quiet hands, and smooth
    Down her patient locks of silk,
Cold and passive as in truth
    You your fingers in spilt milk
Drew along a marble floor ;
    But her lips you cannot wring
Into saying a word more,
    "Yes," or "No," or such a thing :
Though you call and beg and wreak
Half your soul out in a shriek,
She will lie there in default
And most innocent revolt.

IV.

Ay, and if she spoke, maybe
    She would answer, like the Son,
"What is now 'twixt thee and me?"
    Dreadful answer! better none.
Yours on Monday, God's to-day!
    Yours, your child, your blood, your heart,
Called . . . you called her, did you say,
    "Little Mattie" for your part?
Now already it sounds strange,
And you wonder, in this change,
What He calls His angel-creature,
Higher up than you can reach her.

V.

'T was a green and easy world
    As she took it; room to play
(Though one's hair might get uncurled
    At the far end of the day).
What she suffered she shook off
    In the sunshine; what she sinned
She could pray on high enough
    To keep safe above the wind.

If reproved by God or you,
'T was to better her, she knew ;
And if crossed, she gathered still
'T was to cross out something ill.

### VI.

You, you had the right, you thought,
  To survey her with sweet scorn,
Poor gay child, who had not caught
  Yet the octave-stretch forlorn
Of your larger wisdom !  Nay,
  Now your places are changed so,
In that same superior way
  She regards you dull and low
As you did herself exempt
From life's sorrows.  Grand contempt
Of the spirits risen awhile,
Who look back with such a smile !

### VII.

There 's the sting of 't.  That, I think,
  Hurts the most a thousandfold !
To feel sudden, at a wink,
  Some dear child we used to scold,

Praise, love both ways, kiss and tease,
   Teach and tumble as our own,
All its curls about our knees,
   Rise up suddenly full-grown.
Who could wonder such a sight
Made a woman mad outright?
Show me Michael with the sword
Rather than such angels, Lord!

## A FALSE STEP.

### I.

SWEET, thou hast trod on a heart.
   Pass; there's a world full of men;
And women as fair as thou art
   Must do such things now and then.

### II.

Thou only hast stepped unaware,—
   Malice, not one can impute;
And why should a heart have been there
   In the way of a fair woman's foot?

### III.

It was not a stone that could trip,
   Nor was it a thorn that could rend:
Put up thy proud under-lip!
   'T was merely the heart of a friend.

IV.

And yet peradventure one day
   Thou, sitting alone at the glass,
Remarking the bloom gone away,
   Where the smile in its dimplement was,

V.

And seeking around thee in vain
   From hundreds who flattered before,
Such a word as "Oh, not in the main
   Do I hold thee less precious, but more!" . . .

VI.

Thou 'lt sigh, very like, on thy part,
   "Of all I have known or can know,
I wish I had only that Heart
   I trod upon ages ago!"

## *VOID IN LAW.*

### I.

SLEEP, little babe, on my knee,
   Sleep, for the midnight is chill,
And the moon has died out in the tree,
   And the great human world goeth ill.
Sleep, for the wicked agree:
   Sleep, let them do as they will.
      Sleep.

### II.

Sleep, thou hast drawn from my breast
   The last drop of milk that was good;
And now, in a dream, suck the rest,
   Lest the real should trouble thy blood.
Suck, little lips dispossessed,
   As we kiss in the air whom we would.
      Sleep.

### III.

O lips of thy father! the same,
  So like! Very deeply they swore
When he gave me his ring and his name,
  To take back, I imagined, no more!
And now is all changed like a game,
  Though the old cards are used as of yore?
    Sleep.

### IV.

" Void in law," said the Courts.  Something wrong
  In the forms?  Yet, " Till death part us two,
I, James, take thee, Jessie," was strong,
  And ONE witness competent.  True
Such a marriage was worth an old song,
  Heard in Heaven though, as plain as the New.
    Sleep.

### V.

Sleep, little child, his and mine!
  Her throat has the antelope curve,
And her cheek just the colour and line
  Which fade not before him nor swerve:
Yet *she* has no child!—the divine
  Seal of right upon loves that deserve.
    Sleep.

### VI.

My child! though the world take her part,
    Saying "She was the woman to choose;
He had eyes, was a man in his heart,"—
    We twain the decision refuse:
We . . . weak as I am, as thou art, . . .
    Cling on to him, never to loose.
        Sleep.

### VII.

He thinks that, when done with this place,
    All's ended? he'll new-stamp the ore?
Yes, Cæsar's—but not in our case.
    Let him learn we are waiting before
The grave's mouth, the heaven's gate, God's face
    With implacable love evermore.
        Sleep.

### VIII.

He's ours, though he kissed her but now,
    He's ours, though she kissed in reply:
He's ours, though himself disavow,
    And God's universe favour the lie;
Ours to claim, ours to clasp, ours below,
    Ours above, . . . if we live, if we die.
        Sleep.

### IX.

Ah baby, my baby, too rough
  Is my lullaby ?   What have I said ?
Sleep !   When I 've wept long enough
  I shall learn to weep softly instead,
And piece with some alien stuff
  My heart to lie smooth for thy head.
    Sleep.

### X.

Two souls met upon thee, my sweet;
  Two loves led thee out to the sun:
Alas, pretty hands, pretty feet,
  If the one who remains (only one)
Set her grief at thee, turned in a heat
  To thine enemy,—were it well done?
    Sleep.

### XI.

May He of the manger stand near
  And love thee!   An infant He came
To His own who rejected Him here,
  But the Magi brought gifts all the same.
*I* hurry the cross on my Dear !
  *My* gifts are the griefs I declaim !
    Sleep.

## *LORD WALTER'S WIFE.*

### I.

"But why do you go?" said the lady, while both sat under the yew,
And her eyes were alive in their depth, as the kraken beneath the sea-blue.

### II.

"Because I fear you," he answered;—"because you are far too fair,
And able to strangle my soul in a mesh of your gold-coloured hair."

### III.

"Oh, that," she said, "is no reason! Such knots are quickly undone,
And too much beauty, I reckon, is nothing but too much sun."

### IV.

"Yet farewell so," he answered;—"the sun-stroke's fatal at times.
I value your husband, Lord Walter, whose gallop rings still from the limes."

### V.

"Oh, that," she said, "is no reason. You smell a rose through a fence:
If two should smell it, what matter? who grumbles, and where's the pretence?"

### VI.

"But I," he replied, "have promised another, when love was free,
To love her alone, alone, who alone and afar loves me."

### VII.

"Why, that," she said, "is no reason. Love's always free, I am told.
Will you vow to be safe from the headache on Tuesday, and think it will hold?"

### VIII.

"But you," he replied, "have a daughter, a young
    little child, who was laid
In your lap to be pure; so I leave you: the angels
    would make me afraid."

### IX.

"Oh, that," she said, "is no reason.  The angels keep
    out of the way;
And Dora, the child, observes nothing, although you
    should please me and stay."

### X.

At which he rose up in his anger,—"Why, now, you
    no longer are fair!
Why, now, you no longer are fatal, but ugly and hateful,
    I swear."

### XI.

At which she laughed out in her scorn: "These men!
    Oh, these men overnice,
Who are shocked if a colour not virtuous is frankly put
    on by a vice."

### XII.

Her eyes blazed upon him—"And *you*! You bring us
    your vices so near
That we smell them! You think in our presence a
    thought 't would defame us to hear!

### XIII.

"What reason had you, and what right,—I appeal to
    your soul from my life,—
To find me too fair as a woman? Why, sir, I am pure,
    and a wife.

### XIV.

"Is the day-star too fair up above you? It burns you
    not. Dare you imply
I brushed you more close than the star does, when Walter
    had set me as high?

### XV.

"If a man finds a woman too fair, he means simply
    adapted too much
To uses unlawful and fatal. The praise!—shall I thank
    you for such?

### XVI.

"Too fair?—not unless you misuse us! and surely if, once in a while,
You attain to it, straightway you call us no longer too fair, but too vile.

### XVII.

"A moment,—I pray your attention!—I have a poor word in my head
I must utter, though womanly custom would set it down better unsaid.

### XVIII.

"You grew, sir, pale to impertinence, once when I showed you a ring.
You kissed my fan when I dropped it. No matter!— I've broken the thing.

### XIX.

"You did me the honour, perhaps, to be moved at my side now and then
In the senses—a vice, I have heard, which is common to beasts and some men.

### XX.

"Love's a virtue for heroes!—as white as the snow on
    high hills,
And immortal as every great soul is that struggles, endures,
    and fulfils.

### XXI.

"I love my Walter profoundly,—you, Maude, though you
    faltered a week,
For the sake of . . . what was it—an eyebrow? or, less
    still, a mole on a cheek?

### XXII.

"And since, when all's said, you're too noble to stoop
    to the frivolous cant
About crimes irresistible, virtues that swindle, betray and
    supplant,

### XXIII.

"I determined to prove to yourself that, whate'er you
    might dream or avow
By illusion, you wanted precisely no more of me than you
    have now.

### XXIV.

"There! Look me full in the face!—in the face. Understand, if you can,
That the eyes of such women as I am are clean as the palm of a man.

### XXV.

"Drop his hand, you insult him. Avoid us for fear we should cost you a scar—
You take us for harlots, I tell you, and not for the women we are.

### XXVI.

"You wronged me: but then I considered . . . there's Walter! And so at the end
I vowed that he should not be mulcted, by me, in the hand of a friend.

### XXVII.

"Have I hurt you indeed? We are quits then. Nay, friend of my Walter, be mine!
Come, Dora, my darling, my angel, and help me to ask him to dine."

## *BIANCA AMONG THE NIGHTINGALES.*

### I.

THE cypress stood up like a church
   That night we felt our love would hold,
And saintly moonlight seemed to search
   And wash the whole world clean as gold;
The olives crystallized the vales'
   Broad slopes until the hills grew strong:
The fire-flies and the nightingales
   Throbbed each to either, flame and song.
The nightingales, the nightingales!

### II.

Upon the angle of its shade
   The cypress stood, self-balanced high;
Half up, half down, as double-made,
   Along the ground, against the sky;
And *we*, too! from such soul-height went
   Such leaps of blood, so blindly driven,

We scarce knew if our nature meant
   Most passionate earth or intense heaven —
The nightingales, the nightingales!

### III.

We paled with love, we shook with love,
   We kissed so close we could not vow;
Till Giulio whispered "Sweet, above
   God's Ever guaranties this Now."
And through his words the nightingales
   Drove straight and full their long clear call,
Like arrows through heroic mails,
   And love was awful in it all.
The nightingales, the nightingales!

### IV.

O cold white moonlight of the north,
   Refresh these pulses, quench this hell!
O coverture of death drawn forth
   Across this garden-chamber . . . well!
But what have nightingales to do
   In gloomy England, called the free . . .
(Yes, free to die in! . . .) when we two
   Are sundered, singing still to me?
And still they sing, the nightingales!

V.

I think I hear him, how he cried
  "My own soul's life!" between their notes.
Each man has but one soul supplied,
  And that's immortal. Though his throat's
On fire with passion now, to *her*
  He can't say what to me he said!
And yet he moves her, they aver.
  The nightingales sing through my head,—
The nightingales, the nightingales!

VI.

He says to her what moves her most.
  He would not name his soul within
Her hearing,—rather pays her cost
  With praises to her lips and chin.
Man has but one soul, 't is ordained,
  And each soul but one love, I add;
Yet souls are damned and love's profaned;
  These nightingales will sing me mad!
The nightingales, the nightingales!

VII.

I marvel how the birds can sing.
  There's little difference, in their view,

Betwixt our Tuscan trees that spring
   As vital flames into the blue,
And dull round blots of foliage meant,
   Like saturated sponges here,
To suck the fogs up. As content
   Is he too in this land, 't is clear.
And still they sing, the nightingales.

### VIII.

My native Florence! dear, forgone!
   I see across the Alpine ridge
How the last feast-day of Saint John
   Shot rockets from Carraia bridge.
The luminous city, tall with fire,
   Trod deep down in that river of ours,
While many a boat with lamp and choir
   Skimmed birdlike over glittering towers.
I will not hear these nightingales.

### IX.

I seem to float, *we* seem to float
   Down Arno's stream in festive guise;
A boat strikes flame into our boat,
   And up that lady seems to rise
As then she rose. The shock had flashed
   A vision on us! What a head,

What leaping eyeballs!—beauty dashed
  To splendour by a sudden dread.
And still they sing, the nightingales.


X.

Too bold to sin, too weak to die;
  Such women are so. As for me,
I would we had drowned there, he and I,
  That moment, loving perfectly.
He had not caught her with her loosed
  Gold ringlets . . . rarer in the south. .
Nor heard the "Grazie tanto" bruised
  To sweetness by her English mouth.
And still they sing, the nightingales.


XI.

She had not reached him at my heart
  With her fine tongue, as snakes indeed
Kill flies; nor had I, for my part,
  Yearned after, in my desperate need,
And followed him as he did her
  To coasts left bitter by the tide,
Whose very nightingales, elsewhere
  Delighting, torture and deride!
For still they sing, the nightingales.

### XII.

A worthless woman; mere cold clay
   As all false things are: but so fair,
She takes the breath of men away
   Who gaze upon her unaware.
I would not play her larcenous tricks
   To have her looks! She lied and stole,
And spat into my love's pure pyx
   The rank saliva of her soul.
And still they sing, the nightingales.


### XIII.

I would not for her white and pink,
   Though such he likes—her grace of limb,
Though such he has praised—nor yet, I think.
   For life itself, though spent with him,
Commit such sacrilege, affront
   God's nature which is love, intrude
'Twixt two affianced souls, and hunt
   Like spiders, in the altar's wood.
I cannot bear these nightingales.


### XIV.

If she chose sin, some gentler guise
   She might have sinned in, so it seems:

She might have pricked out both my eyes,
   And I still seen him in my dreams!
—Or drugged me in my soup or wine,
   Nor left me angry afterward:
To die here with his hand in mine,
   His breath upon me, were not hard.
(Our Lady hush these nightingales!)

### XV.

But set a springe for *him*, "mio ben,"
   My only good, my first last love!—
Though Christ knows well what sin is, when
   He sees some things done they must move
Himself to wonder. Let her pass.
   I think of her by night and day.
Must *I* too join her . . . out, alas! . . .
   With Giulio, in each word I say?
And evermore the nightingales!

### XVI.

Giulio, my Giulio!—sing they so,
   And you be silent? Do I speak,
And you not hear? An arm you throw
   Round someone, and I feel so weak?

—Oh, owl-like birds! They sing for spite,
    They sing for hate, they sing for doom,
They'll sing through death who sing through night,
    They'll sing and stun me in the tomb—
The nightingales, the nightingales!

## MY KATE.

### I.

She was not as pretty as women I know,
And yet all your best made of sunshine and snow
Drop to shade, melt to nought in the long-trodden ways,
While she's still remembered on warm and cold days --
      My Kate.

### II.

Her air had a meaning, her movements a grace;
You turned from the fairest to gaze on her face:
And when you had once seen her forehead and mouth,
You saw as distinctly her soul and her truth—
      My Kate.

### III.

Such a blue inner light from her eyelids outbroke,
You looked at her silence and fancied she spoke:
When she did, so peculiar yet soft was the tone,
Though the loudest spoke also, you heard her alone—
      My Kate.

### IV.

I doubt if she said to you much that could act
As a thought or suggestion: she did not attract
In the sense of the brilliant or wise: I infer
'T was her thinking of others made you think of her—
                            My Kate.

### V.

She never found fault with you, never implied
Your wrong by her right; and yet men at her side
Grew nobler, girls purer, as through the whole town
The children were gladder that pulled at her gown—
                            My Kate.

### VI.

None knelt at her feet confessed lovers in thrall;
They knelt more to God than they used,—that was all:
If you praised her as charming, some asked what you meant,
But the charm of her presence was felt when she went—
                            My Kate.

### VII.

The weak and the gentle, the ribald and rude,
She took as she found them, and did them all good;
It always was so with her—see what you have!
She has made the grass greener even here . . . with her grave—
                            My Kate.

## VIII.

My dear one!—when thou wast alive with the rest,
I held thee the sweetest and loved thee the best:
And now thou art dead, shall I not take thy part
As thy smiles used to do for thyself, my sweet Heart—
                              My Kate?

## *A SONG FOR THE RAGGED SCHOOL OF LONDON.*

WRITTEN IN ROME.

I.

I AM listening here in Rome.
   "England's strong," say many speakers,
"If she winks, the Czar must come,
   Prow and topsail, to the breakers."

II.

"England's rich in coal and oak,"
   Adds a Roman, getting moody;
"If she shakes a travelling cloak,
   Down our Appian roll the scudi."

III.

"England's righteous," they rejoin:
   "Who shall grudge her exaltations
When her wealth of golden coin
   Works the welfare of the nations?"

IV.

I am listening here in Rome.
　　Over Alps a voice is sweeping—
"England's cruel, save us some
　　Of these victims in her keeping!"

V.

As the cry beneath the wheel
　　Of an old triumphant Roman
Cleft the people's shouts like steel,
　　While the show was spoilt for no man,

VI.

Comes that voice.　Let others shout,
　　Other poets praise my land here:
I am sadly sitting out,
　　Praying, "God forgive her grandeur."

VII.

Shall we boast of empire, where
　　Time with ruin sits commissioned?
In God's liberal blue air
　　Peter's dome itself looks wizened;

VIII.

And the mountains, in disdain,
    Gather back their lights of opal
From the dumb despondent plain
    Heaped with jawbones of a people.


IX.

Lordly English, think it o'er,
    Cæsar's doing is all undone!
You have cannons on your shore,
    And free Parliaments in London;


X.

Princes' parks, and merchants' homes,
    Tents for soldiers, ships for seamen,—
Ay, but ruins worse than Rome's
    In your pauper men and women.


XI.

Women leering through the gas
    (Just such bosoms used to nurse you),
Men, turned wolves by famine—pass!
    Those can speak themselves, and curse you.

XII.

But these others—children small,
　Spilt like blots about the city,
Quay, and street, and palace wall—
　Take them up into your pity!


XIII.

Ragged children with bare feet,
　Whom the angels in white raiment
Know the names of, to repeat
　When they come on you for payment.


XIV.

Ragged children, hungry-eyed,
　Huddled up out of the coldness
On your doorsteps, side by side,
　Till your footman damns their boldness.


XV.

In the alleys, in the squares,
　Begging, lying little rebels;
In the noisy thoroughfares,
　Struggling on with piteous trebles.

### XVI.

Patient children—think what pain
   Makes a young child patient—ponder!
Wronged too commonly to strain
   After right, or wish, or wonder.

### XVII.

Wicked children, with peaked chins,
   And old foreheads! there are many
With no pleasures except sins,
   Gambling with a stolen penny.

### XVIII.

Sickly children, that whine low
   To themselves and not their mothers,
From mere habit,—never so
   Hoping help or care from others.

### XIX.

Healthy children, with those blue
   English eyes, fresh from their Maker,
Fierce and ravenous, staring through
   At the brown loaves of the baker.

XX.

I am listening here in Rome,
    And the Romans are confessing,
" English children pass in bloom
    All the prettiest made for blessing.

XXI.

" *Angli angeli!* " (resumed
    From the mediæval story)
" Such rose angelhoods, emplumed
    In such ringlets of pure glory ! "

XXII.

Can we smooth down the bright hair,
    O my sisters, calm, unthrilled in
Our heart's pulses? Can we bear
    The sweet looks of our own children,

XXIII.

While those others, lean and small,
    Scurf and mildew of the city,
Spot our streets, convict us all
    Till we take them into pity?

### XXIV.

"Is it our fault?" you reply,
  "When, throughout civilization,
Every nation's empery
  Is asserted by starvation?

### XXV.

"All these mouths we cannot feed,
  And we cannot clothe these bodies."
Well, if man's so hard indeed,
  Let them learn at least what God is!

### XXVI.

Little outcasts from life's fold,
  The grave's hope they may be joined in
By Christ's covenant consoled
  For our social contract's grinding.

### XXVII.

If no better can be done,
  Let us do but this,—endeavour
That the sun behind the sun
  Shine upon them while they shiver!

XXVIII.

On the dismal London flags,
   Through the cruel social juggle,
Put a thought beneath their rags
   To ennoble the heart's struggle.

XXIX.

O my sisters, not so much
   Are we asked for—not a blossom
From our children's nosegay, such
   As we gave it from our bosom,—

XXX.

Not the milk left in their cup,
   Not the lamp while they are sleeping,
Not the little cloak hung up
   While the coat's in daily keeping,—

XXXI.

But a place in RAGGED SCHOOLS,
   Where the outcasts may to-morrow
Learn by gentle words and rules
   Just the uses of their sorrow.

XXXII.

O my sisters! children small,
    Blue-eyed, wailing through the city—
Our own babes cry in them all:
    Let us take them into pity.

# May's Love

You love all, you say,
   Round, beneath, above me.
Find me then some way
   Better than to love me,
Me, too, dearest May!

2

O world-kissing eyes
   Which the blue heavens melt to!
I, sad, oversise,
   Loath the sweet looks dealt to
All things.. men & flies —

3

You love all, you say: —
   Therefore, Dear, abate me
Just your love, I pray!
   Shut your eyes and hate me..
Only *me*.. fair May!

           · EBB —

## MAY'S LOVE.

### I.

You love all, you say,
   Round, beneath, above me:
Find me then some way
   Better than to love me,
Me, too, dearest May!

### II.

O world-kissing eyes
   Which the blue heavens melt to;
I, sad, overwise,
   Loathe the sweet looks dealt to
All things—men and flies.

### III.

You love all, you say:
   Therefore, Dear, abate me
Just your love, I pray!
   Shut your eyes and hate me—
Only *me*—fair May!

## AMY'S CRUELTY.

### I.

FAIR Amy of the terraced house,
   Assist me to discover
Why you who would not hurt a mouse
   Can torture so your lover.

### II.

You give your coffee to the cat,
   You stroke the dog for coming,
And all your face grows kinder at
   The little brown bee's humming.

### III.

But when *he* haunts your door . . . the town
   Marks coming and marks going . . .
You seem to have stitched your eyelids down
   To that long piece of sewing!

### IV.

You never give a look, not you,
   Nor drop him a "Good morning,"
To keep his long day warm and blue,
   So fretted by your scorning.

### V.

She shook her head—"The mouse and bee
   For crumb or flower will linger:
The dog is happy at my knee,
   The cat purrs at my finger.

### VI.

"But *he* . . . to *him*, the least thing given
   Means great things at a distance;
He wants my world, my sun, my heaven,
   Soul, body, whole existence.

### VII.

"They say love gives as well as takes;
   But I'm a simple maiden,—
My mother's first smile when she wakes
   I still have smiled and prayed in.

### VIII.

"I only know my mother's love
   Which gives all and asks nothing;
And this new loving sets the groove
   Too much the way of loathing.


### IX.

"Unless he gives me all in change,
   I forfeit all things by him;
The risk is terrible and strange—
   I tremble, doubt, . . . deny him.


### X.

"He's sweetest friend or hardest foe,
   Best angel or worst devil;
I either hate or . . . love him so,
   I can't be merely civil!


### XI.

"You trust a woman who puts forth
   Her blossoms thick as summer's?
You think she dreams what love is wc
   Who casts it to new-comers?

### XII.

"Such love's a cowslip-ball to fling,
  A moment's pretty pastime;
*I* give . . . all me, if anything,
  The first time and the last time.

### XIII.

"Dear neighbour of the trellised house,
  A man should murmur never,
Though treated worse than dog and mouse,
  Till doated on for ever!"

## MY HEART AND I.

### I.

ENOUGH! we're tired, my heart and I.
   We sit beside the headstone thus,
   And wish that name were carved for us.
The moss reprints more tenderly
   The hard types of the mason's knife,
   As heaven's sweet life renews earth's life
With which we're tired, my heart and I.

### II.

You see we're tired, my heart and I.
   We dealt with books, we trusted men,
   And in our own blood drenched the pen,
As if such colours could not fly.
   We walked too straight for fortune's end,
   We loved too true to keep a friend;
At last we're tired, my heart and I.

### III.

How tired we feel, my heart and I!
  We seem of no use in the world;
  Our fancies hang grey and uncurled
About men's eyes indifferently;
  Our voice which thrilled you so, will let
  You sleep; our tears are only wet:
What do we here, my heart and I?

### IV.

So tired, so tired, my heart and I!
  It was not thus in that old time
  When Ralph sat with me 'neath the lime
To watch the sunset from the sky.
  "Dear love, you're looking tired," he said;
  I, smiling at him, shook my head:
'T is now we're tired, my heart and I.

### V.

So tired, so tired, my heart and I!
  Though now none takes me on his arm
  To fold me close and kiss me warm
Till each quick breath end in a sigh
  Of happy languor. Now, alone,
  We lean upon this graveyard stone,
Uncheered, unkissed, my heart and I.

### VI.

Tired out we are, my heart and I.
   Suppose the world brought diadems
   To tempt us, crusted with loose gems
Of powers and pleasures? Let it try.
   We scarcely care to look at even
   A pretty child, or God's blue heaven,
We feel so tired, my heart and I.


### VII.

Yet who complains? My heart and I?
   In this abundant earth no doubt
   Is little room for things worn out:
Disdain them, break them, throw them by!
   And if before the days grew rough
   We *once* were loved, used,—well enough,
I think, we've fared, my heart and I.

## THE BEST THING IN THE WORLD

WHAT's the best thing in the world?
June-rose, by May-dew impearled;
Sweet south-wind, that means no rain;
Truth, not cruel to a friend;
Pleasure, not in haste to end;
Beauty, not self-decked and curled
Till its pride is over-plain;
Light, that never makes you wink;
Memory, that gives no pain;
Love, when, *so*, you're loved again.
What's the best thing in the world?
—Something out of it, I think

## WHERE'S AGNES?

### I.

NAY, if I had come back so,
   And found her dead in her grave,
And if a friend I know
   Had said, "Be strong, nor rave:
She lies there, dead below:

### II.

"I saw her, I who speak,
   White, stiff, the face one blank:
The blue shade came to her cheek
   Before they nailed the plank,
For she had been dead a week."

### III.

Why, if he had spoken so,
   I might have believed the thing,
Although her look, although
   Her step, laugh, voice's ring
Lived in me still as they do.

### IV.

But dead that other way,
  Corrupted thus and lost?
That sort of worm in the clay?
  I cannot count the cost,
That I should rise and pay.

### V.

My Agnes false? such shame?
  She? Rather be it said
That the pure saint of her name
  Has stood there in her stead,
And tricked you to this blame.

### VI.

Her very gown, her cloak
  Fell chastely: no disguise,
But expression! while she broke
  With her clear grey morning-eyes
Full upon me and then spoke.

### VII.

She wore her hair away
  From her forehead,—like a cloud
Which a little wind in May
  Peels off finely: disallowed
Though bright enough to stay.

### VIII.

For the heavens must have the place
  To themselves, to use and shine in,
As her soul would have her face
  To press through upon mine, in
That orb of angel grace.

### IX.

Had she any fault at all,
  'T was having none, I thought too—
There seemed a sort of thrall;
  As she felt her shadow ought to
Fall straight upon the wall.

### X.

Her sweetness strained the sense
  Of common life and duty;
And every day's expense
  Of moving in such beauty
Required, almost, defence.

### XI.

What good, I thought, is done
  By such sweet things, if any?
This world smells ill i' the sun
  Though the garden-flowers are many,—
*She* is only one.

XII.

Can a voice so low and soft
　　Take open actual part
With Right,—maintain aloft
　　Pure truth in life or art,
Vexed always, wounded oft ?—

XIII.

*She* fit, with that fair pose
　　Which melts from curve to curve,
To stand, run, work with those
　　Who wrestle and deserve,
And speak plain without glose ?

XIV.

But I turned round on my fear
　　Defiant, disagreeing—
What if God has set her here
　　Less for action than for Being ?—
For the eye and for the ear.

XV.

Just to show what beauty may,
　　Just to prove what music can,—
And then to die away
　　From the presence of a man,
Who shall learn, henceforth, to pray?

XVI.

As a door, left half ajar
  In heaven, would make him think
How heavenly-different are
  Things glanced at through the chink,
Till he pined from near to far.

XVII.

That door could lead to hell?
  That shining merely meant
Damnation? What! She fell
  Like a woman, who was sent
Like an angel, by a spell?

XVIII.

She, who scarcely trod the earth,
  Turned mere dirt? My Agnes,—mine!
Called so! felt of too much worth
  To be used so! too divine
To be breathed near, and so forth!

XIX.

Why, I dared not name a sin
  In her presence: I went round,
Clipped its name and shut it in
  Some mysterious crystal sound,—
Changed the dagger for the pin.

### XX.

Now you name herself *that word?*
    O my Agnes! O my saint!
Then the great joys of the Lord
    Do not last? Then all this paint
Runs off nature? leaves a board?

### XXI.

Who's dead here? No, not she:
    Rather I! or whence this damp
Cold corruption's misery?
    While my very mourners stamp
Closer in the clods on me.

### XXII.

And my mouth is full of dust
    Till I cannot speak and curse—
Speak and damn him . . . "Blame's unjust"?
    Sin blots out the universe,
All because she would and must?

### XXIII.

She, my white rose, dropping off
    The high rose-tree branch! and not
That the night-wind blew too rough,
    Or the noon-sun burnt too hot,
But, that being a rose—'t was enough!

XXIV.

Then henceforth may earth grow trees!
   No more roses!—hard straight lines
To score lies out! none of these
   Fluctuant curves, but firs and pines,
Poplars, cedars, cypresses!

END OF THE FOURTH VOLUME.

PRINTED BY
SPOTTISWOODE AND CO., NEW-STREET SQUARE
LONDON

www.ingramcontent.com/pod-product-compliance
Lightning Source LLC
Chambersburg PA
CBHW032048230426
43672CB00009B/1524